Different Dads

of related interest

The Complete Guide to Asperger's Syndrome
Tony Attwood
ISBN 978 1 84310 495 7

Kids in the Syndrome Mix of ADHD, LD, Asperger's, Tourette's, Bipolar, and More!
The One Stop Guide for Parents, Teachers, and other Professionals
Martin L. Kutscher MD
With a contribution from Tony Attwood
With a contribution from Robert R. Wolff MD
ISBN 978 1 84310 810 8

Building a Joyful Life with your Child who has Special Needs
Nancy J. Whiteman and Linda Roan-Yager
ISBN 978 1 84310 841 2

Supportive Parenting
Becoming an Advocate for your Child with Special Needs
Jan Campito
ISBN 978 1 84310 851 1

Understanding Your Young Child with a Disability
Pamela Bartram
ISBN 978 1 84310 533 6

Different Dads

Fathers' Stories of Parenting Disabled Children

Edited by
Jill Harrison,
Matthew Henderson
and Rob Leonard

Foreword by
The Right Honourable David Cameron MP

Jessica Kingsley Publishers
London and Philadelphia

First published in 2007
by Jessica Kingsley Publishers
116 Pentonville Road
London N1 9JB, UK
and
400 Market Street, Suite 400
Philadelphia, PA 19106, USA

www.jkp.com

Library of Congress Cataloging in Publication Data
Different dads : fathers' stories of parenting disabled children / edited by Jill Harrison, Matthew Henderson and Rob Leonard ; foreword by David Cameron.
       p. cm.
   Includes bibliographical references and index.
   ISBN-13: 978-1-84310-454-4 (pbk. : alk. paper)
   ISBN-10: 1-84310-454-7 (pbk. : alk. paper) 1. Parents of children with disabilities--Case studies. 2. Father and child--Case studies. 3. Children with disabilities--Family relationships--Case studies. I. Harrison, Jill, 1965- II. Henderson, Matthew, 1975- III. Leonard, Rob, 1969-
   HQ759.913.D54 2007
   306.874'2087--dc22

British Library Cataloguing in Publication Data
A CIP catalogue record for this book is available from the British Library

ISBN 978 1 84310 454 4

Printed and bound in the United States by Thomson-Shore, Inc.

Contents

Foreword

The Right Honourable David Cameron MP has a four-year-old son, Ivan, who suffers from a rare syndrome that includes severe epilepsy and cerebral palsy.

It is a great idea to draw together stories of fathers' experiences in bringing up disabled children.

One of the ways parents manage to cope is to know that others have been through the same experiences. Then you learn that it isn't just about coping – there are positive stories to tell.

I know these accounts will be full of good advice. So I will briefly add just three thoughts. They will be incredibly obvious to those who have already been through this, but they may help those who are starting out.

First, however bad the diagnosis, however desperate you may feel at the time, and however much you feel you will never be able to cope, you do. Things *do* get better. You may well want to thump the first person who says 'Some good will come of this' (I did), but, however unlikely it may seem at the time, in fact they are right.

Second, trust your own judgement. There will be no shortage of advice from doctors, social workers, carers and experts of all kinds. All the advice will be well meaning, much of it will be right, but some will be wrong, and some will be contradictory. The important thing to bear in mind is that you will come to know your child better than anyone else.

You certainly need to listen to advice, but you need also to trust your intuition and judgement.

Third – and this is something that anyone caring for a disabled child or relative should never forget – take a break. Regularly. My family is lucky in that we can get extra care. Many are not so fortunate. But whenever you have the chance to take a break, or to get extra help, make sure you do.

Parents of disabled children are not volunteers. We all care deeply about our children, but that doesn't make us superhuman – and no one should try to be what they are not. An important part of being a good parent is to recognise your limitations, take plenty of breaks, have enough rest and make use of extra help when you can. That is all part of making the best possible contribution to the life of your child.

The Right Honourable David Cameron MP

Introduction

Perhaps you have picked up this book because you have a disabled child or a child with special educational needs yourself. Perhaps you are working in, or training to work in, the 'caring professions' and want to know more about working with fathers. Perhaps you have a friend, colleague or family member who is the father of a disabled child.

In this book, fathers of disabled children talk directly about their feelings and needs, and tell their own stories in their own words. We hope that, whatever the reason you have picked this book up from the shelf, it will help you.

The UK charity Contact a Family, for which two of the authors work, has many years' experience of working with families with disabled children. When we run fathers' social events, we find that dads enjoy meeting one another and talking about things that are often deeply personal, displaying none of the reserve and reluctance to engage with one another for which the British are justifiably famous.

At one of our events, one father described his son's exclusion from school that day and how his wife had forced him to come along to the fathers' evening. He said that he had only come to avoid the argument that they would have if he stayed at home. Despite his initial reluctance to come he later said, 'This has been a release, someone has let me say how I feel and understand how I feel.' Another said, 'I just wanted someone to burden it all on to. But you find that people's eyes just glaze over. I just wanted someone to listen. I didn't want people to chip in with advice. People shouldn't feel they have to.'

Other dads commented: 'She goes to all the meetings and I just turn up when I'm needed or told that I'm needed'; 'I go to the meetings when things are bad and I have to act tough to get what we want.'

They all talk about the difficulty of managing home life and working life, and the lack of understanding by employers. They talk about lack of sleep as a significant element of their working and caring lives. They feel that this affects all their relationships and, most importantly, their relationship with their partner. They all recognise they have lost friends over the years and sometimes have no idea how to make new ones.

Many speak of the isolation they feel from other parents they come into contact with – either extended family members or families of their non-disabled children's friends. Many feel that they are often at the receiving end of hurtful, unhelpful or even prejudiced comments:

> We have only just this month received a Christmas present from last year because they won't come round and see us. They know what a difficult time we are having at the moment but they still expect me to do all the running around after them because I am 'not working'.

They all feel that they are fighting 'the last civil rights movement'. Their children are being denied access to education, leisure and friendships that other families take for granted: 'We have had to fight for everything. We have been to tribunal twice and to the doors of the High Court just to get a mainstream education for our child.' They also feel that it is their duty as dads to take this fight on: 'We are not just going to sit back and let them ignore us.'

It generally takes the dads no time at all to connect with each other and one commented, 'I've more in common with these dads than mates of mine I've known for years.' Another said, 'We have all made a connection tonight, even though our children are all very different. It's so good to sit and talk to people in the same boat.'

They do say that some things are changing for the better with the emergence of 'parents' rooms' and 'parent and toddler groups', for example. However, they think that the image of parent support groups is still 'female' and that many dads do not 'get' what support groups are all about: 'It's very easy to make excuses and there is always something else that needs to be done.'

Another commented:

> Coming along to a group like this is admitting that your child has a disability. I think many dads I know locally are still at a stage of denying that there is anything wrong. One particular dad spends

all the time working on his farm to avoid confronting problems at home.

One dad asked whether we could set up a dads' chat page on our website, and felt that many men would be more comfortable seeking support in that way.

Several fathers also told us that they would greatly value a book in which they could read other men's stories. We agreed. Knowing how valuable the dads had found our meetings and hearing others speak about their lives, we wanted to create a permanent collection of stories from men of all backgrounds, for those of you that don't have a local fathers' group or would rather not go to one.

We used a combination of inviting fathers to submit written accounts and interviewing and recording others who felt less confident about their ability to articulate their feelings on paper or whose typing skills were not up to the job. Some names and locations have been changed at the dad's request. The men whose stories follow live in different parts of the UK; they are of different ages and backgrounds; they are from white, black and Asian ethnic backgrounds; some are married, others are living together with a partner, widowed, separated or divorced; some are working and some are full-time carers; some are biological fathers and others are step-, foster or adoptive fathers.

Each account ends with a description of the condition that affects the child, taken from the Contact a Family Directory of Rare Conditions or the National Support Group website for the particular condition. The information included was correct as from summer 2006. Because medical understanding moves on, however, we have included a link to the relevant web page for up-to-date information. The final chapter looks at how to start to get the support you need. At the very end of the book is a glossary of some of the medical and colloquial terms used in the text.

The dads in this book all talk in some detail about their own personal situation, their feelings, and how they coped and still cope with being a 'different dad'. We hope their stories are helpful to you. If you are a dad with a disabled child, please know that you are not alone. Across the UK alone there are over 700,000 men who know how you feel. They share similar hopes and fears, and have gone through many of the same struggles and sacrifices. We also hope this book will give 'new' fathers of disabled children an insight into the journey ahead – in short, the advice that many of the men who tell their stories here never got. Being a father is every bit as important as being a mother, albeit in a very subtle and different way. You are all heroes in your own right.

John

John lives with his wife and two daughters in a small town in Scotland. John has been married for ten years now. It is a scenic part of the world with nice walks and beautiful views of the surrounding hills. John has been a full-time procurement engineer for a multinational computer firm for the last 15 years and his wife has worked part time in a local chemist for 12 years. His two-year-old daughter, Rhiannon, has arthrogryposis multiplex congenita.

In 2001 we had a new addition to the family with the arrival of our daughter Abbie, now four. Abbie is a character and keeps us firmly on our toes; a wonderful girl who very much lights up our lives. We decided that Abbie would benefit from having a brother or sister, so we were delighted to hear that another would be on the way in early 2004.

We were pretty much enjoying family life and looking forward to the birth of our second child in 2004. Donna had taken care with her eating, took folic acid, drank lots of water, and alcohol was completely taboo. In fact she had given that up prior to conceiving. You could say that she was doing all she could from her end, to try and bring about the best start for any new child coming in to the world.

In 2000 we had experienced a miscarriage so the doctors monitored my wife's pregnancies closely. Throughout this pregnancy we had regular hospital visits, with scans every three to four weeks. In all we were set for what was expected to be a natural birth as the prenatal scans and test results were all as expected. However, near the end of the pregnancy we were informed that the baby was in a breech. As such, the consultant would monitor and try to turn the baby. If unsuccessful, we would have no option but to go through Caesarean section. After several attempts, there was no joy so, to my wife's dismay, it would have to be a Caesarean. While this would be welcome to some women, my wife was gutted.

We were apprehensive about the whole thing given that we had to travel outwith our own town to another hospital with better facilities. The date was set. It was surreal going to bed the night before and trying to sleep. Eventually we would awake in the morning knowing that we were off to hospital to come back with another new addition. We did feel apprehensive about the whole thing – a natural birth can just happen, yet this was almost planned.

Once at the hospital we went through the normal procedure. To be perfectly honest I didn't like the hospital full stop! The cleanliness, standards and staff didn't appear to be what we were used to. That was my gut feeling at the time. Eventually we were called downstairs. Donna was given her epidural and I was sanctioned to the doctors' room to change into something appropriate for the theatre. I felt good at this point after the surgeon made some funny comments about my gown. Shortly after, I was invited in to the theatre, where I was located (head side of my wife). The doc said that I wouldn't remember a thing if I was at the 'other end'. I couldn't agree more. We both felt really happy and were looking forward to getting it over and done with. Anyone who has ever experienced a Caesarean section will know what I mean.

Anyway, after some pulling around, our latest addition was pulled out into the world. It only took about 20 minutes. As part of a natural birth, the baby is brought directly to the mother for skin contact, but there was some hesitation. I couldn't help but notice the baby's hands were turned inwards, almost deformed in a way. I had a gut-wrenching feeling and didn't really know what to expect. I knew something was wrong. Donna couldn't really see, as there was a screen in front of her, but I could tell something wasn't right. The midwife, surgeon and consultant grouped together around the baby. While they were chatting, one of the nurses came over to talk to us. She was chatting away as if everything was OK and I suppose she was buying some time. I asked her if all was OK, but I could see that something was definitely wrong with the baby's hands. At this point we still didn't know if we had a baby boy or girl. It was completely weird. At the birth of Abbie I was crying with delight, yet I was gutted inside at this point, knowing that something was wrong. But what? The nurse told us that they had to do some routine stuff given that the birth wasn't natural. Apparently they needed to clear the baby's lungs of fluid. Normal practice. After what seemed like an eternity, they brought our daughter over wrapped in a towel. We had to ask the sex.

Our daughter was now in our hands, but only briefly. At that point we could both see her hands were deformed and that she had club feet. We mentioned this to the consultant and registrar, and they patted me on the back and said don't worry, we are looking into this. They did not know what it was at the time.

Things seemed to go really quiet for a bit and we were really nervous. We just didn't know what to expect. It truly was gut wrenching. One minute you are on a complete high and then it is swept away from under you. I will always be grateful and feel blessed to have such a beautiful daughter but I couldn't understand or comprehend what was happening in front of me. This was not in the script, it wasn't expected and no one was prepared for it. Even the consultant was in shock as this was something that he hadn't seen before. We were soon moved into a room adjacent to the theatre. A nurse would be present at all times while in there. I just wanted to tell her to go for a walk as we wanted some privacy to chat, but that wasn't to be – they knew that something wasn't right and wanted to be sure that there was cover at all times. In fact, I didn't even feel that the nurses were sympathetic in any way at all – they just hung around.

At this point my head was like a toy shop. What's wrong, how, why, what do we say to people? How am I supposed to react? I didn't know whether to cry. It was very stressful; I felt sick and I was worried for my wife. She was hurting and trying desperately not to show any emotion. Donna and I were deep in shock about it all. I kept saying that it'll be all right, let's just wait and see what they say. About an hour had passed and no one had been in to inform us what was happening. It seemed like time had stood still. Eventually we got five minutes alone. We then held our daughter and decided that the name Rhiannon was the most appropriate.

I'll never forget holding Rhiannon for the first time and seeing her reaction looking back. She had the awareness of a six-month-old baby with her head upright looking back. It was strange, it just seemed like she was aware of what was going on. This does sound strange, I know, but she didn't come across as a baby just born. She just seemed far too alert to the world around her.

Eventually, about two hours after the birth, we had decided that I should call the folks who had been waiting anxiously: both sets of grandparents, some friends, work colleagues, etc. I wanted to be so happy calling these folks. While I was happy, I was also very sad that there had been complications and that I didn't know what they were. What do I say to people?

My mother and father would be the first to know, so I called them. My first reaction was to tell them that it was another girl, a sister for Abbie, a second granddaughter that weighed 6 lb 9 oz, that she had a full head of black hair and that we named her Rhiannon. It was a very positive start but eventually I had to explain that there were some complications. I explained that we didn't know what the complications were but we would have to wait and see. I stated that there was nothing to get worried about at this time, let's just wait and see what happens, it might be nothing. I didn't really realise it at the time but I was starting to get some strength about dealing with this. My mother and father were gutted too, I could tell, but they were trying to be positive. Several other calls were to follow and my voice was getting hoarse, my throat was dry and I was fed up with explaining it all.

Our immediate families were upset, and my work colleagues and friends didn't really know what to say at this point. Donna's mother was also upset, concerned for her daughter and, in a way, I guess she could sense how Donna was feeling.

Eventually we were moved back to the maternity ward and placed in a private room. Rhiannon, Donna and I were all alone. It was good to get some space, but we felt isolated too. Why are we in a room of our own? In a way it was good, but it was strange given that there were loads of mothers walking around with new babies and they were very happy. We felt envious and sad that we were hidden away.

Eventually I was asked to take Rhiannon for various X-rays of her hips, legs, arms, spine, etc., to determine if there were any deformities. This was a real awkward time as she was screaming and naked to the world. A new baby should not be exposed to this. The results did not flag anything at that time. I was just there as the father caring for my daughter, awaiting the results of the consultant's analysis.

Time passed and I eventually headed off to collect Abbie. Donna and I had planned to tell Abbie together about her sister the following day; we would all be together as a family sharing the news with Abbie, and letting her see her sister for the first time. As such, the plan was for me and Abbie to stay away until the next morning, but I was called back to the hospital that night to hear my daughter's diagnosis. The consultant had visited while I was out and he gave a bleak outlook for our daughter. It was explained that she may never walk, would have limitations and that there was still much uncertainty. There could be complications, they needed to do tests. My wife was faced with this on a day that was to be so special. It was too much to take.

In a way I have never felt comfortable when visiting hospitals prenatal, for a birth or otherwise relating to a pregnancy. I feel that fathers are ignored on occasion and almost not part of the conversation. In my experience, in some cases, the father is left out. However, on this occasion, the consultant would soon visit the room again and assess Rhiannon. He didn't know exactly what was wrong at first but he did have an idea. The condition would later be diagnosed as arthrogryposis multiplex congenita (AMC), although thankfully Rhiannon did not have the most severe form of it. He did ask me to go away and come back with questions. Needless to say I pulled loads together.

You see, we were faced with something completely new to us – we had never heard of this condition. It was something new that we had to live with and yet we felt fortunate in a way and that we could have been worse off. It was a weight off our shoulders – it could have been worse. For sure there are children worse off.

Like many people, I didn't think it would happen to our daughter. It was a good pregnancy, nothing showed up. It was just routine. We were going around enjoying our own life and didn't expect this to happen. To that extent it changed my outlook overnight as I now had to deal with something completely new. We all had to deal with something new!

Rhiannon is still a baby meeting most of her development skills. However, she has many physical limitations for her age. Her range of movement is very limited and she cannot feed or stand independently. There are many new people in our lives now and, to a certain extent, we are very comfortable with the new routine. It truly was very difficult at first: we had to deal with so much uncertainty, testing, waiting on results, not to mention all the hospital appointments.

On a personal level I am very much part of everything that goes on within Rhiannon's life. I wouldn't want it any other way. I wouldn't have it any other way! Thankfully the professionals that deal with Rhiannon are very understanding, and provide excellent support and guidance to my wife and me. We are forever indebted to Rhiannon's paediatric consultant from the children's hospital. He really does have her best interests at heart and has an open mind to our views. He also kick-started a lot of the medical support and really does provide a first-class medical practice/clinic.

Not all medical professionals are the same, though. They really need to understand that fathers are very much part of their child's 'whole life', and should therefore promote all aspects of their treatment and encourage fathers to get involved and/or keep them informed. Likewise, fathers should ensure that they are involved and that their views are heard at all times.

My advice to fathers who learn about their child having been born with a disability is: don't panic, it's not the end of the world. It's never easy learning that your child has a condition or disability but we need to deal with it. Frank as it may seem, we do need to be there for them and to ensure that they are getting the best support available to them. If a father has just learnt that his child is disabled then I would urge him not to give up, to be strong and to question things. Sometimes it's not as bad as it may seem.

If you are unhappy about anything then it's best to question it or get a second, or maybe even third, opinion. Sometimes doctors are known to predict the worst possible outcome, as we experienced when my daughter was diagnosed. However, we later found out that things weren't as bad as first predicted. I could have strangled that consultant for painting such a bleak outlook and giving such a negative view. I was incandescent. On the flipside, we see so many positive things from our daughter's development and we are glad that things aren't as bad as first predicted. At first our life as a family was in turmoil, there was so much uncertainty, but we have come a long way and have seen many improvements. Time is a great healer, but get the best help, listen and be very, very patient. For sure your life will change.

One thing that might bother folks at first is people looking or staring. I always say to my wife that people will stare anyway, it's part of their curious nature. Don't always assume or take it the wrong way if someone is staring at your child. The majority of the time they will just be concerned. Sometimes the parent (father) can take this personally but please don't, just ignore it.

Almost two years on I still ask myself the same questions, but you have to be positive. I often ask what can be done. Early diagnosis was essential so that the relevant treatment could start as quickly as possible. To assist in that diagnosis a series of tests were carried out to eliminate other distinct conditions. For example, investigations on the central nervous system, a head scan, a muscle biopsy, X-rays of the spine, pelvis and the limbs involved, as well as the bladder.

In our case physiotherapy was the immediate concern as it plays a leading role in the treatment of arthrogryposis. A programme of passive stretching, while the baby's tissues are still supple, needs to be introduced as soon as possible to try to increase the range of movement in the stiff joints. This is coupled with the use of splints to maintain a good position in the limb. The success of repositioning joints and limbs that can be achieved by persistent physiotherapy cannot be overemphasised.

We were also put in touch with a local physiotherapist who would later teach my wife and me the various techniques necessary so that we could continue the daily programme at home in between hospital visits. In the first few months Rhiannon was also placed in plaster casts and had some minor corrective surgery to complement the work of the physiotherapist and paediatric consultant.

The future is bright. We have a healthy daughter, a beautiful daughter of whom we are very proud. She has helped change our lives for the better and she is coping with things in the way that she can. Almost two years ago the outlook was bleak and uncertain, but we now know what road we are taking and we are all living with the disability together.

If able-bodied people had the same determination as disabled folk, then we would all be winners.

About arthrogryposis multiplex congenita

Arthrogryposis multiplex congenita (AMC) is not a diagnosis but a descriptive term used to describe a baby born with joint contractures affecting at least two different areas of the body. The joints may be fixed in a bent or straightened position. It is believed that such contractures may result from one of several processes that cause the unborn baby's limbs not to move properly at the time the joints are being formed. These processes fall into the following main categories: problems with the nerve supply, the muscles, the connective or supporting tissues, and external factors such as the blood supply to the baby or the shape of the womb. Approximately 1 in 5000 babies are affected.

For further information see www.tagonline.org.uk.

Phil

Phil and his family live in north-east England. Phil gave up paid work to become a foster carer. He and his wife have one birth daughter, who was almost 14 when they fostered Cameron, who is two and has multiple disabilities.

At the age of 34 I had it all – the salary, the house, car, the expense account, the business trips, the suits, a successful marriage to a gorgeous wife who also had a successful career. I had a super-talented, beautiful, well-rounded teenage daughter, flying high in one of the region's best private schools. All the things to which people aspire – I had them all.

Except for the fact that there was something missing, life was good. There was a void, a gap and the problem was that I wasn't sure what that missing component was, and the more I searched, the more frustrated I became. Things continued to slide downhill until eventually I slipped into a state of depression and needed to take time off work to organise my thoughts. I was snapping at my angel of a wife, shutting her out, blaming her for heaven only knows what. She, to her infinite credit, remained constant and sympathetic to my ever changing needs and demands. What I had done to deserve her I will never know!

After a time I began to see a glimmer of understanding, the mist began to lift and things steadily became clearer. I was beginning to identify the root cause of my unhappiness: I wasn't making a difference. When I was out with the lads, I wouldn't discuss my work for fear of boring the pants off them, so meaningful to the world was my contribution. I was embarrassed by the inanity of it all, the pointlessness, the sheer lack of worth in what I contributed to the world. I contacted human resources and expressed my desire to accept redundancy terms; in April 2004 I found myself jobless and, wow, did it feel good. My wife suffered a job loss, too, so here we were: both jobless and, to my amazement, happier than we had ever been.

We decided to take time out of our lives simply to rediscover ourselves as people, and relax and enjoy life. To think about the future, to discuss our options and to re-evaluate our lives was also a part of the process. During this time we found our calling, or at least I did! The decision we reached was to become foster carers. By then our daughter was nearly 14 and was deeply involved in the process.

To wilfully invite a stranger into your home to evaluate, judge and question every aspect of your life to date is a scary thing, but that's what we did; it was necessary if we were to be approved as foster carers. The next six months were to be the most enlightening of my entire life; to go through this evaluation process was the most soul-searching, emotional, life-enhancing experience I could ever imagine. It opened doors the mind keeps locked, it found places in the heart that were kept hidden. In a nutshell it flays you open for the world to see the real you. I embraced this with all I had and at the end of it all I felt cleansed and ready for anything. Mostly, though, I came to a profound realisation: that I had played only a peripheral part in my daughter's parenting, contributing where I felt I could, but mostly I had been happy just to let my wife get on with it. This hurt me more than I can say, but I accepted it and decided things would change from now on.

My wife decided to go back to work and this meant that I went forward to the approval panel as the main carer. We flew through approval – initially as short-term carers, to get our feet wet, with a view to becoming long-term carers should we be suited to the life.

Following this, I started to educate myself in the subject of what positive parenting actually looked like and the theory behind it. I became absorbed in all those TV programmes that show families in turmoil where professionals intervene; you know the ones. I also became engrossed in books on the subject and read many eye-opening stories of stolen childhoods, neglect and abuse, as I knew that the likelihood of us having young people live with us who had suffered this kind of start in life was high.

Over the course of the next year, we had a number of different children come to us, each with one thing in common: they'd all had a lousy start to life. We laughed, cried, played and worked with them all. I know that all of these kids left our home having had a very positive experience, many coming back two or three times at their own request, and I was doing it, I was really making a difference. I was doing what I should have done with my own daughter years ago. I was satisfied and I was happy.

In late summer 2005, our link worker casually mentioned a baby who was in need of care. I asked her to tell me more. She was apprehensive about going into any details as my father-in-law had recently been diagnosed with cancer. He was a very ill man and I was spending most of my free time with him. My link worker felt that, given our circumstances, it wouldn't be fair to us to be expected to give this child the care he needed. However, I was insistent.

This baby was desperately poorly and in dire need of help. Over 30 carers had been given this child's details and none of them was prepared even to discuss the possibility of taking him into their lives, such was the complicated nature of his case. We learned the following:

- his name was Cameron and, at 15 months old, he had never left hospital
- while in hospital, he was parentally neglected
- he was born with a congenital heart defect, namely hypoplastic left heart syndrome, meaning only one side of his heart was functioning
- he had only one working lung
- he had no spleen, meaning he was extremely vulnerable to infections
- he'd had open-heart surgery five times
- he had global neurodevelopmental delay
- he had hydrocephalus – fluid on the brain – giving him a disproportionately large head
- he had a pacemaker
- he was unable to eat or drink, having lost the instinct to swallow
- he was permanently fed via a naso-gastric tube

- he had had MRSA numerous times and any infection/virus could take his life
- he was a prime candidate for sudden death due to heart failure; he shouldn't be alive, in truth
- his physical development was delayed
- he had regular medicinal needs
- he had no experience of just being a child.

The most important thing we learned, however, was the simplest of all: *he needed us.*

There was no need for discussion; we looked at each other and the decision was made. We wanted to meet him and we set off for the hospital. When we arrived, we both immediately felt deep despair. In a side cubicle, all alone in a large iron hospital cot, on his knees and tummy, with his hands tucked under him, rocking back and forth and banging his head off the bars of the cot, was Cameron. Every documentary that I'd ever seen showing children abroad in dilapidated orphanages or squalid hospitals came rushing back to me. It was at this instant, we looked at each other and we knew: this little fellow was going to change our lives and family make-up for ever.

Meeting followed meeting and a care plan was devised, wherein I would spend a month or so attending the hospital at all hours of the day and night, getting to know Cameron, his care regime, his medications, gaining in-depth knowledge of his condition, his abilities and restrictions, and also, of course, for my commitment, attitude, effort, etc. to be scrutinised and reported on (this was never actually part of the agreement; however, we knew it was happening).

I got to know the nurses, doctors, social workers, etc., and on the whole I was impressed with their level of commitment and the effort they made to answer the 20 million questions I asked on a daily basis. I've heard since that I was a pain in their collective backsides, but they were also delighted to have someone show so much commitment and effort to learn what needed to be learned.

During this month, a much deeper understanding of issues surrounding Cameron was gained. Two that I found very difficult and frustrating were very simple: Cameron would not give eye contact, nor would he demand attention. Can you imagine, a child of that age constantly giving you clear messages that he wanted to be left alone?

While in hospital it was difficult to play, so I took the bull by the horns and insisted on taking him outside to the park. The nursing staff were a bit reticent – he hadn't done anything like that before! They relented, however, and to say a new little boy began to emerge is a huge understatement. Cameron's little face lit up, his inquisitiveness was bewildering, and when he looked at me and smiled, then laughed as I pushed him on a swing, you could have given me a billion pounds and I wouldn't have exchanged how that made me feel!

That month spent in hospital was long, hard and very trying. Every task relating to Cameron's care was set as a reminder in my mobile phone and it never seemed to stop going off! I didn't realise it at the time, but my way of caring for Cameron had been to break the day into a series of tasks. That way I suppose, I couldn't get it wrong – a definite hark back to my project management days.

In the autumn, Cameron was discharged from hospital into our care and our lives together were to start in earnest. We quickly got into our routine, but the number of visitors became increasingly overwhelming. Doctors, nurses, social workers, play therapists, occupational therapists, dieticians, speech and language therapists, support workers, community health visitors, as well as Cameron's parents, all became part of my new life and I wasn't fully prepared for that – had I been, I would have replaced the front door with a turnstile!

At times, our angel of a daughter was often left out of our thinking, particularly mine. She was doing well, and didn't need me as much as other people did, so I didn't worry about her. I am ashamed to say that was my thinking. Of course she needed me, though, I just didn't see it at the time.

When the court case was scheduled Cameron's parents decided to concede and the full care order was done and dusted within half an hour. I am not sorry to say that I literally whooped! Cameron's parents' visiting privileges were drastically reduced and I was back in control of my home. My wife went to work, our daughter went to school, and Cameron and I were at home. The drugs, the cleaning of the horrid secretions (I don't think I've mentioned that to this point): Cameron was and still is prone to projectile vomiting, seriously explosive diarrhoea, phlegm, mucus and anything else you care to imagine. I took care of all the professional appointments, and there were lots! I did all the things that a team of nurses had previously done, as well as trying to help Cameron developmentally (often getting nowhere). When my wife came home of an evening, I would tell her what had happened that day, often with exasperation, frustration and annoyance, and retire to the conservatory to just be by myself and let her deal with the evening shift. I often found that I'd had enough and just wanted to be alone, to relax, have a beer and play some computer games. I don't think my family fully appreciated this and would come and try to talk to me when all I wanted was peace and quiet.

I was beginning to find, also, that my protectiveness and sense of *getting it right* where Cameron was concerned was becoming an obsession, it had to be my way – deviate at your peril. I realised that my thoughts were constantly on him, but felt no need to alter my way of thinking. I was dreaming about him regularly and every tiny detail had to be the way I demanded. Every minute of every day, tasks had to be performed to exacting standards and timing – my strategy for dealing with the situation. If Cameron died, then I couldn't be faulted. As in my previous job, if the project failed it wasn't due to my overlooking a small detail. My wife showed the patience of a saint with me, offering inconspicuous little bits of advice here and there, but still allowing me to maintain the control of Cameron's care that was so important to me. A clever lady indeed!

My agency had been, since the beginning of our relationship with Cameron, trying all ways to get us (me especially) to agree to let Cameron be 'looked after' on occasion by other carers. My reaction was always a resolute no. He was part of our family and we wouldn't farm him out to people we didn't know; we would deal with it. But on the day of my father-in-law's funeral we relented. He was out of our care for a total of three hours, and he never will be again. He had vomited on himself and hadn't been changed, and his bottom hadn't been cleaned properly following a heavy soiling.

In early January 2006, things took a severe downturn. One morning, Cameron turned very blue (compared to his normal blue). He was listless, lethargic and extremely sleepy. My immediate response was to get a community nurse to come and monitor him. To their infinite credit, someone was at our home within half an hour and it became instantly clear that his state of health demanded immediate attention. I wrapped him up, bundled him into the car and raced towards the hospital. Feeling desperately sick, I parked the car on double yellows, left the doors open and ran with him as fast as my little legs would carry me.

When we got on to the ward, it hit the fan in a big way. The nurses and doctors all knew Cameron, of course, but the reaction of the first nurse said it all, she literally went ashen: I swear I could see the colour drain from her face. She ran to the nurses' station, picked up the phone, and that's when all hell broke loose. My stress levels rose, and Cameron picked up on this because he, too, became increasingly agitated and nothing I did could calm him. They attached him to a vital signs monitor, which showed a pulse of 190 and a blood oxygen saturation level of 30 per cent – a level that is considered too low to sustain life. Within minutes we were surrounded by expertise. Cardiologists, heart echo mechanics, nurses, a resuscitation team, ECG and EEG people, people poking and prodding, taking blood, mucus, blood pressure, installing cannulas (long needles into a vein), people giving oxygen…

Have you ever seen *Casualty* or *ER* when they bring in a crash team? Well, this was worse. I have to tell you, I have never, ever been more afraid in my entire life; and, all through it, Cameron was looking directly into my eyes, beseeching me, please – make it stop, make them go away; but I couldn't. I knew I had to let these people do their work. Cameron and I must have shed gallons of sweat during all of this. However, the staff had taken control within minutes of us arriving and I was scared but reassured, heartbroken, but strangely calmed and, above all, fiercely protective. They gave me all the information I wanted, which meant I was able to feel more relaxed, which Cameron felt too.

When he went to sleep, I just sat there staring at the poor little man. I suppose I was in a daze. I had known this could happen and thought I was emotionally prepared for it, but I wasn't, not even close. After a day or so, the results came back: he had contracted bronchialitis, which can be fatal, so I was told to expect the worst. The chances were high that he would not survive.

I was living on tenterhooks and became very inward; but Cameron pulled through against the odds, very slowly, but after a week he was discharged from hospital – much to our huge relief.

I'm not sure how, but this episode gave me a better feeling about Cameron: if he could survive this, then maybe he wasn't quite as fragile as I had myself believing. If anything, I became a lot more relaxed regarding his regime, less protective and overbearing. It had taken a lot of time, but I now felt more relaxed, and instead of looking at the illness first and then at the needs of the child, I began to see that we had a gorgeous little boy who needed to be allowed to be a person, rather than a medical case. My task-centric way of doing things, and my overprotectiveness were getting in the way of Cameron being allowed to enjoy life to the fullest, and this was something he richly deserved.

Cameron has been poorly on a couple of occasions since then, and has attended clinics where I have been told that his heart is having to work so much harder as he grows and becomes more active. He is unquestionably at the stage when his heart could just stop functioning at any point. It is difficult to live like that, not knowing what you are going to wake up to, feeling tense and living with constant worry. I still find myself slipping into inwardness as I ponder the future, but, through it all, I have my better half. She keeps my head straight and encourages me to do all the 'normal' things with Cameron. I continue to learn, and we continue to go forward as a family with a difference – a very special difference.

Finally, if I were to be asked to give advice to other dads in a similar situation, I would offer the following tips:

- Educate yourself – do not wait for others to tell you, find out as much as you can about the condition and what to expect.
- With education comes empowerment. Take control and call the shots; don't allow yourself to be overwhelmed.
- Adopt a collaborative approach with health professionals; try not to have an 'us' and 'them' attitude.
- Seek help. There are lots of support groups, community-funded respite and assistance to be had.
- Communicate – share how you feel, particularly with your loved ones.
- Be a pain in the backside; make sure you get done what you feel is right for your child and your family. Don't accept no.
- Take time out for yourself. Do something you really enjoy doing occasionally, and don't feel guilty about it.
- Allow the child to be a child; try to see past the disability.
- Trust others. Don't try to do it all yourself.
- Listen to advice. You don't have to accept it, but it may have validity.

About hypoplastic left heart syndrome and hydrocephalus

Hypoplastic left heart syndrome

Hypoplastic left heart syndrome (HLHS) is a complex congenital heart condition that occurs in 1 in 5000 children. The syndrome is a collection of malformations on the left side of the heart:

- mitral atresia/stenosis
- hypoplastic left ventricle
- aortic atresia/stenosis
- hypoplastic aorta.

This collection of malformations is incompatible with life, and without treatment most of these children will die within the first week after birth.

Surgical treatment is presently offered in a limited number of paediatric cardiac centres in the UK. The complexity of the surgery requires a dedicated, experienced team approach. The overall survival rate of all children starting down the surgical treatment path is that 60 per cent will still be alive at five years of age.

For further information see www.lhm.org.uk.

Hydrocephalus

Hydrocephalus is commonly, but inaccurately, known as 'water on the brain'. A watery fluid known as cerebro spinal fluid (CSF) flows through narrow passageways in the brain from one ventricle to the next, out over the inside of the brain and down the spinal cord. CSF is continuously absorbed into the bloodstream and the amount of pressure is kept within a narrow range. If the flow of fluid is obstructed at any point, it accumulates in the ventricles, causing them to enlarge and compress surrounding brain tissue. In babies but not older children or adults the head will enlarge. The most common causes of hydrocephalus in children are infections such as meningitis or toxoplasmosis, premature birth, head injury or a brain tumour.

For further information see www.asbah.org.

Andrew

Andrew and his wife live in Yorkshire. His five-year-old son, Mark, has oesophageal atresia. Mark has one older brother, Christopher. Andrew is a postman and his wife is a legal secretary.

Mark was born at our local district hospital. The doctors and midwives knew that he had possible problems as previous scans had revealed that Mark had no fluid in his stomach. This was an indication of oesophageal atresia.

Mark was born four weeks early and weighed 4 lb 14 oz. After a few hours in the local hospital, Mark was transferred to a larger hospital in a city ten miles away, under the care of a paediatric surgeon. I remember seeing Mark in a hospital cot connected to all these bleeping machines, and then meeting the surgeon and being told that he would be operating on Mark in the next couple of weeks. I remember looking at how small Mark was and how tall the surgeon was and thinking how can this man operate on Mark? Mark then spent the next couple of weeks on the neonatal surgical unit, hooked up to all sorts of machines. The overriding feeling I remember is one of complete helplessness. I had no control over what was happening or what was going to happen. I could not take the pain away for my little boy or my wife, and everything was out of my control. Mark was born with long gap oesophageal atresia and tracheomalcia.

When we both found out that there was a possible problem with Mark, and Catherine had to give up work, I told my employers, Royal Mail, of the situation. I had to give up work too when, two months before

Mark was born, Catherine became too poorly to carry on looking after Christopher and the house. Royal Mail has in place a 'family-friendly' attitude towards any problems that may occur, so I was supported throughout my time off before Mark was born. In total, I had to take about six months in one continuous period off work until Mark was discharged from hospital. One of my main worries was that I would not receive my full basic pay, but Royal Mail gives you six months' full basic pay as standard. I had to take this time off as sick/compassionate leave. Because Mark's condition was so complicated none of the managers or people in charge at Royal Mail had any idea how much stress we as a family unit were under.

Two weeks after his birth, Mark had a delayed primary repair to try to join the two ends of his oesophagus together. I remember waiting as the hours ticked by. The surgeon rang us at home and said that he had managed to join the two ends together but that it was very tight and that there might be a need for future dilatations. This was, in fact, the case and this happened every fortnight. The surgeon then came to see us again and explained that, because of the reflux Mark was experiencing, this was not helping the need for dilatations and that it was advisable to have a fundoplication. This was carried out two months later. This seemed to help with Mark's oral feeding and finally he was allowed home, three months after his birth.

Life at home was very stressful and there was always the overriding feeling of anxiety in case Mark choked or his breathing and swallowing became impaired. After six months of continuing dilatations, the surgeon said that he thought it would be in Mark's best interest to have a gastric transposition, which involved moving Mark's stomach up into his chest. This was a major operation, which would involve Mark spending more time in the intensive care unit, but we had no option as his quality of life was the only thing that mattered. I remember waiting at home, as we could not face the wait in the hospital – over 14 hours whilst Mark was in surgery – until the surgeon telephoned us to say that the operation had gone well. I remember wondering how much more could Mark's little body take and how much more could we, as his parents, take emotionally.

Thankfully, the operation went well and after recovery Mark was transferred back to the local hospital to help us gain confidence in looking after him before he came home. Unfortunately, this was delayed because Mark stopped breathing whilst there and was transferred back to the larger hospital where he was kept under observation in the intensive care unit. The surgeon, again, recommended another operation, which was carried out shortly before Mark's first birthday. Mark was fed by a jejunostomy tube for a long time, initially during the day and night and then eventually during the night only.

Because of what had happened to Mark and the feeling of total helplessness, I slipped into a serious depression when Mark was approximately two years old. I was advised by my doctor that I should not attend work for another six months to help me to come to terms with what had happened and to recover. Royal Mail was not as understanding of the depression, however, and I had to attend various interviews to assess when I would be able to resume normal duties at work. My colleagues at work could not have been more understanding or supportive. It's at times like these when you really find out who your true friends are. Although I still have days when the depression feels like it could come back I just think of the support of my family and colleagues at work who have helped me. Royal Mail has tried to put me on a Stage 1 sickness (there are only three before dismissal), but so far I have managed to stay off them. However, there is nothing built in to the working structure that allows for this type of thing.

Although it has been a long road, Mark's intelligence and love of life never ceases to amaze me. I am very proud to be his dad and he has an amazing amount of inner strength.

I look back on those dark days still with sadness as some feelings do not disappear, but it does get better with time. You think in the early days that the future is uncertain, and it is, but as time goes by you seem to learn to deal with the condition that your child has and you move on and learn to deal with situations as they arise. I hope that this helps anyone who is beginning their journey, gives them strength and hope. Life does get better – it just takes time, patience and a lot of love.

About oesophageal atresia

Oesophageal atresia (OA) is a rare congenital condition of the oesophagus (food pipe) that affects newborn babies.

With OA, the oesophagus forms a closed-off pouch that prevents food from reaching the stomach. Prior to corrective surgery, this pouch can fill up with food and saliva, which can eventually overflow into the baby's trachea (windpipe), entering the lungs and causing choking.

For further information see www.tofs.org.uk.

Rob

Rob is a teacher and lives with his wife, who is a doctor, and family in the north-east of England. His son, Matthew, is six and was infected with cytomegalovirus as a baby.

Matthew has given me a shape to my life that was somehow missing. His disability has made me reconsider the whole path and pattern of my life. What is more, it has been for the better. I have changed my lifestyle and working pattern to accommodate Matthew, and in the process I have been able to see how rich and wonderful life is without waiting until I retire and it is too late. I now see beauty in things I would once have walked straight past without a moment's notice. All this because Matthew was born with a disability! This does not mean that I have fully come to terms with him and his disability, far from it. Days spent with him, whilst caring and loving, are intense and hard both physically and mentally. The type of care that he needs from me will change form and motion as he gets older and his needs fluctuate. This is my story, and relates where I am as a person now in the present day, a fraction of the way down a very long road that is Matthew and my life. I have created ten 'lessons' that may help anyone else in their journey of either understanding or coping with a disabled child.

Matthew was born 'normally' on 24 July 2000: 24/7 is how I remember it, and how ironic that now seems in retrospect, perhaps even a little perverse. On reflection, although he seemed 'normal' to me at the time, I remember a feeling of something not quite right. It was such a small feeling and I just dismissed it at the time. What did I know about childbirth? After a few months his feeding had not been good at all and my wife, Helen, had pushed past the GP and health visitor – who had reassured us that he was a 'difficult feeder because he is a boy, and you know what boys are like' and that it would be OK with time – and secured a hospital appointment, which included a blood test 'just in case' there was something unknown to us. The day we were told by the specialist that Matthew had an infection called cytomegalovirus (CMV) my wife broke down. Because she was a doctor it hit her straight away. It didn't hit me. Sure, if Helen reacted like that it must be serious, but medication would clear it up and it would be fine, yes? No. Matthew was put on an antiviral drug, which after some time did the trick and removed the virus from his body, but it was too late: the damage was done.

We were now collecting specialists. It was shortly before Christmas that one of them gave what I now look on as one of the few pieces of advice that really made a difference. It was from our social worker; she told us that it would take about one year just to survive and come to terms with our life. If we could survive that year then our family, marriage and relationship would remain intact. How right she was! That year was the most torrid in my life; it is testament to Helen and her will and determination that our family is still intact, and I am eternally grateful to her for that.

That was *lesson one*: stand by your partner no matter what. You can draw strength from each other in times that are bad. You both share a common goal: the well-being of your child. Listen to each other and support each other, *talk!*

Angry. That would be the best way to describe my wife. Passive. That would be the best way to describe me! Whilst my wife got going with caring for Matthew – researching, speaking to colleagues, nagging specialists – I did the opposite. I buried my head in the sand. After all, if I could become the breadwinner in the family I was doing the natural thing. Hunting and gathering whilst my wife did the woman's job: looking after the kids. So I threw myself into work. I was a fairly successful teacher, training to become a head teacher and applying for deputy headships. The future looked very good career-wise. But as I spent more time obsessed with my job and getting a promotion, the wheels were slowly coming off at home. I wasn't giving my family the support and, more importantly, love it required. I was also quite firmly in denial. Helen was getting counselling to help her cope, but because I seemed OK no one except Helen had suggested that I needed help too. Helen had pushed for me to get some counselling through the GP but I'd been almost relieved to find out how difficult it would be to get support. Although I did not realise it, this was the first barrier that I had to face in my journey. It wasn't until I broke down soon after that the journey really started.

I remember the day vividly. I was doing less at home than ever before and, although I did not realise it, my anxiety levels were high. I was at school at the time and, thankfully, not teaching. A colleague of mine was asking me for something (I cannot even remember what, it was that insignificant a request!) when I snapped. The final straw had been put on the camel's back and I broke down. I cried like I'd never cried before; it just flooded out. Thankfully for me that member of staff knew what to do and shuffled me straight into the head's office. He dropped everything and came to my side immediately. This was the moment that changed my life, and I owe it to this most wonderful, compassionate man, head teacher and humanitarian extraordinary. What he did was simple yet so difficult. For the next hour he let me cry, let me curse, let me say whatever I wanted to say. Then he said these simple words:

> I have no idea how you have lasted this long before this happened. But I know one thing – you must go and be with your family, because they are the single most important thing in your life and they need you now. They need your love and you need theirs. I do not want to see you back in this school until you and your family are sorted out, safe and happy. That may take a week, a month, a year; I do not care how long. Go home; that is where you belong now.

This was *lesson two*: your family comes before anything else, your job, your personal desires and goals, your social strata, whether you like it or not. I was to learn over time to like it very much!

Life was about to begin again for me, but that isn't the end of the story, it is not all happy ever after. I had some major decisions to make and some very big bridges to build. It wasn't just 'Honey I'm home! I'm here to save you and the kids!' because, after all, they had sort of left me behind. They needed to save me, and there were still a lot of tensions between Helen and me. The immediate term was about Matthew and getting him as healthy as possible. I could now attend medical sessions. I had some compassionate leave and was allowed time off to go to appointments. I then learnt that, at these meetings, if you don't ask you do not get told!

This became *lesson three*: don't be dictated to by professional people. Ask questions, enquire, and push for more information and care. As the saying goes in the north-east, 'shy bairns get nowt'! Know your rights and what you are entitled to by pushing and not taking no for an answer.

Things were starting to happen now. I still had difficulties and issues with home life, but we had moved house to a bigger property (which needed a bit of work, but had space and land), and generally we were getting the hang of Matthew's needs. This all helped, but he was in and out of hospital a lot with chest infections, and he had fits that we were gradually getting under control with medication. The real stress was just coping and getting a bit of respite care (this is yet another issue I will come to later). During this time I really learnt who our friends were. Helen had a very close support group of friends she had known from school. I was quite jealous of this on two levels. Not just the fact that she had such good close friends and I didn't, but also that she seemed in my mind to have more trust in them than me. This was compounded by some of my friends just 'vanishing' into thin air. Sure they had their own lives, but some just drifted clean away. (I guess I was a bit to blame myself as I have never been the most communicative by nature, and I am a bit of a loner. Nonetheless, many old friends drifted into obscurity.)

The plus side was that a close circle of good friends, who accepted Matthew and me for who we were, was emerging. One old colleague, Paul, would call around after work almost every Friday, just to say 'hi' and have a beer, chew the fat and listen. And that was the key: just listening, not trying to sympathise because in his words he 'couldn't even begin to understand' how I felt. That sort of friendship was, and still is, gold dust to me.

This became *lesson four*: be true to yourself and your true friends. A true friend will listen and will be there whenever they can. This will sound awful, but don't waste time chasing old lost friends who have just 'vanished' because, if they really value your friendship, they will come back to you in your hour of need.

My relationship with Helen was still on a roller coaster and Christmas was approaching fast. It was nearly a year since Matthew had been diagnosed and it was fair to say that, although we had come a long way, we were still within that critical year that our social worker had talked about. That Christmas, as if to proclaim our new house open, we had decided to have both of our immediate families over. The day itself actually passed off quite well, but the days leading up to it, and the evening after everyone had just about gone, were stressful and charged with tension, to put it mildly! Christmas evening for me was a watershed in our relationship. We had argued quite hard, said things we both didn't mean and threw the odd object! With hindsight it is humorous, but at the time it wasn't pleasant. It was then I realised that the greatest asset in my survival was the one thing I had been abusing for the last couple of years: Helen. Although things did not change overnight I made a real effort to be more understanding; in short, compromise was the order of the day. This was no longer about me, it was about 'us'. I realised that our feelings were rarely in synch. The days I was up, she would be down, and vice versa. These were the times when we needed to lean on each other. I'd been good at leaning; now I had to be prepared to be leaned on.

From this came *lesson five*: your partner is your closest ally. Not just your best friend and lover, but your sounding board and your support. This only works if you reciprocate for your partner; it is a 50/50 deal!

This tied in closely with my decision finally to go part time and give up my pipe dream of deputy headship and in turn headship, but not without one more throw of the dice. I had already started to have my doubts and was sure that I probably didn't have what it took. I had dropped the equivalent of one day, to take Matthew to a parents' group at a special school we were interested in him attending and to take a break and help at home generally. But then, when our head had retired and our current deputy was promoted to his post, it left the deputy job free at my school. I made up my mind. If I got this one it was meant to be, if I didn't then it wasn't and I would give up on management. Deep inside I knew I wouldn't get the job and I was not at all surprised when someone else was offered it. At the end of that year I dropped to three days. I had been lucky. The governors at the school had been very supportive and approved it straight away. However, the new head was very keen that I would go back full time; he even asked me less than one month into starting on my new part-time hours if I would go back to full-time work. I just don't think he realised that our difficulties at home would be permanent, not over in a couple of months. This made me realise how lucky I had been to that date: first, in realising I should work part time, but, second, how lucky I had been that my 'managers' had simply allowed it to happen. At this point I knew my time in this post was coming to an end. The new deputy was putting pressure on the whole staff and the goodwill was evaporating. The family atmosphere of the school I'd loved working at had gone.

I had a new ally in a charity, Contact a Family, and in particular a wonderful, colourful friend: Kathy. Kathy had first met Helen when she arrived at an event, as Kathy puts it, 'as angry as sin' and has been an enormous support ever since. They had all manner of information about working rights, to name but a few. I wrote to the head and governors reiterating my decision to stay part time in order to be with my family. Meanwhile Matthew (after a minor tussle) had got a place at our chosen school and it meant I could help more at home whilst Helen got her career back on track working three days a week too. Armed with this information and renewed confidence that I was in the right, my part-time status was approved without any problem. The governors had come up trumps again! It was, however, too late: I knew that enough was enough – the school just wasn't the same for me. Don't get me wrong, it supported me generally and the staff were fantastic at their jobs, but the new regime offered no room for flexibility, and Helen and I knew I had to get out. At the time we were overlapping working days and had a third baby on the way. I decided to take the plunge and resign, do supply teaching for a bit and wait for the next best option.

This brought me to *lesson six*: know your employment rights. There are plenty of employers that will apply far more pressure on than mine did. On the whole, my situation was very well supported and understood; many I have spoken to have not been so lucky. Find out your rights and stick to them!

We – or more precisely Helen – were getting rather good at pushing for things. We had managed to get Matthew to the school we wanted, got him a purpose-built bed and were (thanks to Helen's ability to get her head around the form!) on the higher-level Disability Living Allowance. There were still things that rankled, though. Respite care was one. It seemed as if the only way you could get this was if your child was about to die of some terrible disease or illness. We did fleetingly have a care worker visit for one night a month to be with Matthew (his sleeping is awful to this day and every night we get up frequently to be with him). However, it was not working. The care worker from social services had no nursing or childcare training, and her understanding of Matthew – through no fault of her own – was minimal. She even managed to burn Matthew's milk despite the milk being in a bottle in the fridge with the microwave timer set (all she had to do was put it in and press start). She did not last long. We discovered direct payments and, using two close friends and former nursery workers that knew and had worked with Matthew, employed them to have him for a few hours each weekend. It still came back to Helen pushing for it, though, filling in masses of tax and employment forms, and has been far from simple! It was almost like dealing with all the different services right back at the start. Although we had changed as people, the system had not. You still had a fight with most things, and that was even with a certain amount of 'insider knowledge' thanks to Helen's experiences in the medical profession.

So this is *lesson seven*: try to find out exactly what you are entitled to. Get help getting it and don't take no for an answer. There is a lot out there you are entitled to that for some reason is kept secret! Realise, though, that funding for some things is index-linked to your income. This means, in practical terms, that although our income isn't high, we get nothing at present. Our modified people carrier was paid for with our own money, and it wasn't cheap!

So where did that leave us? I've talked a lot about me, and little about Matthew. His needs are profound, and he is getting older. With the freedom my new working hours had brought I felt able to do more for him and around the house. I started to understand my son more. It had taken until his third year for this to happen, so I felt there was some time to make up. A moment I will never forget was administering him medicine to stop him fitting one night that Helen was at work. I was terrified because I knew if I got it wrong or it didn't work, it would be a hospital job, possibly even a 999 job. It worked, and I felt an enormous level of pride and achievement in myself. I had developed, I had read the signs of what was happening, and I had responded to the needs of my child, albeit in an extreme situation. It was a mixture of joy, relief and sadness that I'd needed to 'treat' my own child and had got it right.

Matthew, for all his difficulties, is a happy child in the main. He loves being in a child carrier on my back. This is great because it's too physical for Helen so I feel that this is something I can do for him that no one else in the family can. In a silly way that satisfies my 'macho' side, which still has microscopic issues with being a 'child carer' and not a 'hunter-gatherer'.

Mealtimes are hard because he cannot feed himself and suffers discomfort when he eats. I tend to feed him most of the time, which can be frustrating, and sometimes I lose patience. My eldest daughter keeps me straight here – telling me to be patient in her own way! All this keeps me sane most of the time. This leads me to coping. Although it seems that pouring yourself into your new extreme family life is the way, all of us need to escape – even if we have a 'normal' family. For me, my two days a week in my new job as a school sports coordinator are a great release; but my real 'reality buster' is a weekly game of rugby, which helps me let off steam! The rugby club at Ponteland is also a fantastic family club, and they have taken Matthew to their heart. At one presentation evening they gave me a portrait of Matthew and myself that one of the senior members had painted; I was so moved. I recounted to the members and their families there about being out shopping earlier that week and, for the first time ever, noticing people staring at Matthew. It didn't upset me, I just found it odd. I then said that the beauty of the club was that no one judged you, you were who you were and you were part of one big family. One member grabbed me after this. His son was deaf and played for the first team; he said that was exactly it: no one judged him for being deaf! He was a good rugby player and part of the club's family, and that was the important thing. A wonderful moment for both of us.

This takes us to *lesson eight*: you need to make time for yourself, even if it is just to have a bath on your own for half an hour, or to go out for a drink with your partner, or to let off steam playing a sport (in my case badly!). It also leads on to *lesson nine*: it doesn't matter about other people's opinions; what matters is what close friends and family think, and that they understand. They will only understand if you tell them about it.

New horizons lay ahead. Not just with the development of Matthew but the dynamics of our family. We had decided to have another child. There was a distinct risk of the same thing happening a second time. We decided for various reasons we would do it. Having another child would also give Sophie, our eldest, a 'normal' sibling. It sounds awful but that was quite a motivation. When Helen became pregnant we did not want even to contemplate anything going wrong, and although we had lots of extra scans and were dealt with wonderfully by the medical staff, it was never really a reality to us. That was until Charlotte was born, healthy and normal. What a relief, to put it mildly!

Now we are five we have as much happiness as I could ever have contemplated. My journey still continues as Matthew gets older. I dare not dream of the future and what it holds. I still catch myself having morbid thoughts and bemoaning my fate in a selfish way: 'Yes, Rob, get it into your head that he is not going to score the winning try for England in the Rugby World Cup Final, because he'll never even play rugby!' Those thoughts can eat you alive, and need to be dismissed.

Which leads to the *tenth lesson* I've learnt: each person, in his or her own way, has a hard life, but there is always someone worse off than you. Celebrate and enjoy what you have, don't rue or regret what you do not have. Live life to the full and enjoy every minute you have on the planet!

About cytomegalovirus

Cytomegalovirus (CMV) is a common virus, and about 50 per cent of the population of Britain have been infected with it at some time. Frequently the infection passes unnoticed or there may be mild flu-like symptoms. In the UK about 40 per cent of women are susceptible to CMV at the time of pregnancy. The chance of the baby becoming infected is about 40 per cent. Over 90 per cent of infected babies have no signs of anything wrong at birth. Some of these infants may go on to develop hearing loss over the first five years of life. A small proportion of infected children can have pneumonia, liver disease or neurological problems including cerebral palsy and developmental delay.

For further information see www.cafamily.org.uk.

Kash

Kash lives in the north-east of England. He is a widower, bringing up his three children alone: daughters Amani and Ayla and a six-year-old son, Faris, who was born prematurely at 24 weeks.

To try and comprehend the loss of bringing a child into the world with a disability is almost impossible unless you have suffered that fate yourself. However, if that wasn't enough, what happened to me and my family next would destroy almost anyone. I survived, and this is my story so far.

I was born in England but returned to Pakistan with my family when I was two. I then came back to England and school when I was nine, with very little English. It would be a difficult start for any child, but hard work and a supportive family brought me success. I met and fell in love with an English girl. Despite her being English, our families eventually respected our love and we got married. We had two beautiful girls and it all seemed like a fairy tale. Only one thing was missing: a little boy that would extend the male line, so important to many Asian families. When my wife soon fell pregnant again our hopes were high.

Our excitement about the new baby was tempered when he arrived at 24 weeks, weighing only 1 lb 2 oz. It was clear that the delight of this new baby boy would be replaced with a fear that he would even survive. Baby Faris was now on the special care baby unit. His lungs were weak and underdeveloped, which meant lung infections followed.

Two months after being born, and after multiple 'attempts' at incubation, he was fitted with a trachie (tracheotomy tube). It would not be until six months after his birth that Faris went home for the first time. It seemed like a small ray of hope but it didn't last long. Within a month Faris was back in hospital with yet another infection. It was so bad that doctors feared the worst; indeed on one occasion a doctor spent two hours respirating Faris with a bag. The local hospital had come to a dead end. They told us they had a new 'possible' solution: extra corporeal membrane oxygenation (ECMO) treatment, which can help some children with very severe lung disease, but it was only available at a hospital in Leicester, many miles away. Faris was airlifted there almost straight away.

Despite this trauma Faris and the rest of the family eventually returned home, with many mixed feelings. At just ten months old Faris was starting to defy the odds, and seemed at the point of survival. However, the treatment had left its problems. Faris would have his trachie for two years (according to the medical staff) and he would be developmentally delayed in many aspects as a result of being so sick (trachies prevent the child from developing any vocal skills). It still seemed like a mountain for my family to climb. Would we ever be normal again?

Not long into our new lives, we decided to try and bring a bit of normality and fun back, and I decided a day trip was needed. Alton Towers was the planned venue, and the whole family plus Faris's medical equipment set off. We hoped it would be a tonic for all of us, but the trip became a living nightmare.

Whilst there, my wife had an asthma attack – not something the family wasn't used to as she had suffered from the condition for years; however, it turned out to be more severe than we first realised and she was airlifted to hospital. To compound matters, Faris became unwell almost simultaneously, and had to be taken to another specialist hospital. The conundrum for me now was where to go: to my son's or my wife's side. I made the difficult choice. As Faris was known to the hospital from the ECMO treatment, I rushed to the hospital my wife had been taken to and eventually got to her side. She died soon after.

Many people would start to challenge their own existence at this point, but with the speed of everything that happened, I did not have time to dwell on matters. I had to become not just the father of a disabled son, but the mother and father of all of my children. I had to learn to be a mother before anything else! Despite wanting to give up completely, and coming close to giving up on many occasions, a basic instinct kicked in: the care of my children. This overrode any feelings of loss for me; those feelings were now pushed firmly to one side in order for me to care for my children.

To this day (five years later), because of all that has happened, I have not had any real chance to grieve for my wife. My trials and tribulations have meant giving up everything: a promising career and family home life – all that has been turned on its head. Needless to say I have learnt to deal with things almost by trial and error. I took on the burden of Faris's care to a point where I probably know more about his condition and how to deal with it than most doctors. It has been a steep learning curve. My frustration, however, soon began to boil over; I was and still am a time bomb waiting to explode.

I am the first to praise some of the positive support I have received. However, on many occasions I have had 'brushes' with social services and medical professionals. All I really wanted was support to help me access the right information about what was best for my son. On many occasions I have found myself in meetings where my ideas were dismissed and given no respect. This created a wall, a barrier that I could cross only if I had the right answers delivered in a sensitive manner. Support and help, which was surely a right, was all I wanted.

Despite all this, Faris started to grow, and with the love of his dad and his sisters, he came through his difficult start. He still had many problems, however: the trachie meant he had no verbal communication and his developmental delay, both physically and mentally, was becoming apparent.

However, as with all children, he was growing up and I decided to find a nursery place for him, to encourage his social skills and to gain some form of respite for me from the 24-hour care that my son needed.

I approached many nurseries to try and find a place for Faris. He needed some positive interventions to help him catch up. Mainstream state nurseries would not take him due to his complex needs and dependency on oxygen. This lack of service for many parents of children with special needs is a real issue that still grates on me to this day. So I took on the fight and called a multi-agency meeting to try and sort it out. It became very frustrating when no plans were made in meeting after meeting. It got to the stage where I instructed a solicitor to attend the next meeting to support me. It created a 'them and us' situation, which would grind on before we eventually found a nursery prepared to accept Faris, except that the staff had no experience and training. The difference this time was that this group of people genuinely wanted to help and learn. They set clear goals for Faris and learnt how to cope with his condition, mostly with training delivered by me! I spent 11 months in the nursery, training staff and building their confidence so that they felt comfortable with Faris and, in turn, any other disabled child they might care for in the future.

It was clear that without my drive, together with the sheer determination of Faris's 'angels' who looked after him, he would never have had the opportunity to develop in the way that he did. That is not to say it happened overnight; there were many 'fights' with management to get to that stage. I did what I could to support the nursery, raising funds to provide it with computers, and even setting up a sensory room.

With typical fight, I went to Great Ormond Street for advice on my son's care, and discovered that his treatment was well behind the latest research and development. I discovered that I had been changing his trachie daily when weekly with proper equipment would be all that was needed. Naturally I challenged his medical staff, and more friction and fights ensued, though eventually I won through.

My life began to transform when the nursery fulfilled its promise to get Faris walking and feeding orally. As with anyone who has done their best for their family, I would die for them. But things move on, and Faris would soon need to move to school properly. The special school that he was due to attend was good and true to its word and, as a result of good communication with me, understood what Faris needed and how he should be looked after. He is now thriving at school.

I have this simple advice for people in my position: question everything, don't take no for an answer; ask for help and clear information about everything, especially benefits (I haven't been able to work since Faris was born); don't wait for a response – pester for answers as sometimes you will get lost in the system; know your rights and find out more from good sources. I also try to champion the rights of people who have limited knowledge of the system, the ones that need help now, not tomorrow.

I am close to my wife's family despite the cultural differences. They love the children but are reluctant to look after Faris as they, quite understandably, fear his condition and feel they could not cope. (This is the case with many elderly relatives.) They still remain highly supportive of me, though, treating me as a son rather than a son-in-law. My own close family offer support in a more traditional way – cooking and cleaning for me when possible – however, I still fear how I will bring up two young Asian daughters who traditionally would have been looked after closely by their mother. I find this almost as hard as looking after Faris and his 24-hour medical needs.

I am determined that people should not have to find things out the hard way, as I did. Too much was left to chance in my case, and were it not for my determination I would not be in the position I am in now. It may be down to my resilience and belligerence that I still have my family and a portion of my sanity, but it has come at a cost. I still cannot be in my home on my own without my children; the memory of my wife makes it too hard. My life is like climbing a steep cliff: you cannot see the top of it; you look back and can't see the bottom; you are too tired to climb and you have your family attached to you by a line, depending on you for their safety; no one helps you – it's groundhog day, a limbo state…a sleepless repetitive life waiting to crack, waiting to fall. A hard way to live, and this is reflected in the lack of respite care that I get.

Although I have developed an aggressive attitude (which I find is the only way to get what my family needs), beneath it all I am deeply caring. The brash attitude and fighting nature is in some respects a defence mechanism that gets me through the day. I now work as a voluntary representative for Asian families for Contact a Family North East. I pass on all my life experiences and offer support to others, and the work I do allows me the freedom to plan my day around my family.

Despite my anger at the system, which I feel has failed me in many ways over Faris's care, I still value anyone who has helped me and my family in any way, however big or small. When challenged about fighting the system legally, I always refuse, as I do not want to burden an already creaking system. All I want is the here and now. I want support for me and my family. I want the care I feel my son deserves, and I want my daughters to have the chance to grow up in a normal, healthy way. I want the time to mourn the loss of my wife, which, in nearly six years, I have yet to have the chance to do.

For me, the time bomb may still explode.

About prematurity

Preterm infants are those that are born before 37 weeks' gestation. With modern perinatal and neonatal intensive care it is now possible for many babies born prematurely to survive. The majority of these babies do so without significant long-term problems; a few babies are now surviving from as little as 23 weeks' gestation, although at these extremes there is more concern about long-term problems and their developmental outcomes.

For more information see www.bliss.org.uk.

Simon

Simon, his wife Diane, and their children Paul and Jenny live in Oldham in the north-west of England. Paul is 13 and is on the gifted and talented register at school. Diane works as a computer programmer and Simon is a tutor with a local adult education service. Their seven-year-old daughter, Jenny, has autism.

When Jenny was two years old we began to explore what was different about her. Being the dad of a disabled child is a strange thing: you are quickly aware of the tension and sacrifice the child is going to require, you know that you are in this for life, but I never felt any rejection towards Jenny or any anger about it.

When we decided that we wanted another child, I was quietly confident for a bright future. We have brought Paul up with the opportunity to develop his natural intelligence and his easy relationship with adults.

I was confident and proud of what my new daughter would achieve; I had a series of tapes ready to record her language as it developed in the stages defined by language expert David Crystal. Alas fate, life, God, whatever or whoever, has a habit of playing tricks. Two years from the first few noises I was still recording babble and puzzling over when the first word would arrive. The language delay was becoming more and more obvious. The professionals from preschool special needs, and others, must have had their suspicions, but you prefer to listen to the older generation and friends who like to tell you that 'she'll be OK', 'they all develop at different rates'. People will give you little anecdotes about children who said not a word until their fourth birthday and then treated their parents to a rendition of some complex tome.

Then suddenly Jenny was diagnosed with autism. She was never going to catch up and she was not going to be normal, she wasn't even 'a bit slow' or a 'giddy kipper' (an excitable person); she was profoundly disabled, with a lifelong condition, a handicap that would mean she could never take a full part in society. For the next three years, from two and a half to five and a half, Jenny became defined by her autism. There were statements to be sought, benefits to be claimed, behaviour strategies and learning plans to put in place. You have to hand things over to social workers, paediatricians and even volunteers; your child is not your own and, no, you do not always know what is best. For example, when should you ask a child questions? If they are autistic much of the wisdom says not for a long time.

Gradually, I have got Jenny back. She's becoming more than a series of issues, problems and targets. Jenny is now understandable and under-standing. She is speaking English like a foreigner and has no in-built grammar: 'zebra, black and white, want to go see, mummy and daddy and Paul and Jenny' translates as a request to go and see the film *Racing Stripes* at the cinema with all the family. She also frequently mixes up words like 'chicken' and 'kitchen', 'Cathy' and 'cafe'. She has great enthusiasm and often re-enacts scenes from Disney for us, now that she can make herself understood more easily. She frequently gets the wrong end of the stick! But her smile and her charm are usually able to get her out of trouble. How long this will last I don't know, with me it will probably be for ever!

I find Jenny's disability frustrating at times; we went to see *Beauty and the Beast* live at the Manchester Opera House. After five minutes we had to go; Jenny just left the theatre. However, she did want to stay in the foyer watching the grainy images on CCTV. Now she still asks to go to see *Beauty and the Beast* live, again. It is impossible to bend her will; if she doesn't want to do something she won't do it. Yet most of the time Jenny is just a fun person to be with; you have to fit in with what she wants and do as she says, but gradually she is getting some empathy. She told me off the other day for shouting at Paul.

You have to modify things a bit. Taking Jenny to large supermarkets to do the shopping was a nightmare: she would disappear almost imme-diately and I would have to abandon my trolley to chase her round the shop, always getting that sickening feeling that someone might take her.

Now we go to a much smaller supermarket: you can see where she is all the time, there is only one way out and the entire process is quick enough to keep Jenny involved. It is a bit bizarre that she keeps trying to pick up chickens to eat since we are vegetarians: it makes you realise how much chicken is eaten in films.

I am far more tolerant now of naughty children. In fact, when we go to the cinema I hope there will be some noisy children getting up and running to the toilet every five minutes, as this will distract people from the rambling, running, highly inaccurate commentary coming from next to me. In Pizza Hut I hope for a rowdy party of kids to stop people looking at Jenny collecting cheese and pepper jars, climbing on the chair or messing with the blinds. Everything seems to happen at high speed; there is little time for reflection and thought. Decisions have to be made quickly and stuck to. Even now I will say 'Would you like to go upstairs for your bath now?' and be surprised when she says 'No.'

In some ways having Jenny has made me a less tolerant person. I can't stand those who mock her; I often suspect even children in the school are playing 'chase' with her because she is different. I get cross with older people who grumble about Jenny if she is misbehaving. I think of them as a generation where 'mental handicap' was out of sight and that they live in the dark ages. The same goes for other nations; I watch documentaries where people in other countries are locked away to become institutionalised and sometimes die of neglect when their original problems were not much different to Jenny's. I am tempted to think of this whenever an issue about that particular country comes up.

Constantly I think of the future. All my political and social ideals have become focused on Jenny's disability. I become angry with business and government, as it insists that everyone must be flexible and have good skills in maths and English if they are to be employable. What use is that to Jenny? Many people with autism fitted perfectly well in pre-industrial society; useful roles requiring concentration or attention to detail or repetition could be found. It seems people with disabilities are to be further marginalised at the very time when they are becoming more visible. They are either expected to work 40 hours a week for the minimum wage, or to be on a treadmill of endless courses and social activities, with little control over their lives.

I think that this is so important to all of us. We should not try to control others' lives. It was not me who made Paul an academic success, just as it wasn't me that made Jenny have autistic spectrum disorder (ASD). I realise all we can do is try to give as many rights and responsibilities to our children as we can. With Jenny we will just have to do that in a more considered way.

I feel the need to work as many hours as possible in order to bring in money; this means that when I come in from work I find it hard to motivate myself to get involved with committees and support groups. When you do go to events they tend to be mum-dominated and it is difficult to know quite what tone to take in conversation – men and women do have different topics they prefer to discuss. When talking to other men without experience of children with disabilities, children don't dominate the discussion. If there were events that couples both went to, that would give dads more opportunities to build relationships with each other. I found a recent dad's evening in a pub interesting and useful. With a men's group that has been set up for that purpose I can feel at ease. We all have lots of ideas and experiences to share. I still like to keep most of the feelings to myself, but sharing incidents, accidents and ideas with other dads is always a good experience as they can empathise more than the male friends that I have had for 20-plus years.

My advice to a dad whose child has had a recent diagnosis? Read as much as you can, find all the information and experiences of other people and then realise that most of it has to be reinterpreted in the light of your child. Channel your energies into positive things: campaign for better service if that is your skill, or focus on your own child's needs, which is what I did. Try to find things funny that otherwise would be frustrating or depressing; on the other hand, don't be afraid to challenge other people who treat your child with less respect than she or he deserves. It is important that the distant problems don't swamp the simple pleasures of the present: the first bit of eye contact, the genuine laughter, the first garbled communication that you understand, and the look on their face when they realise you are on their wavelength. Never forget that you have a child not a problem.

Would I change things now? I wouldn't! I love Jenny the way she is, with her funny language, her peculiar manners and sense of fun, none of which she would have if she wasn't autistic. So thank you fate, life, God, whatever or whoever, for the privilege I have been given.

About autism

The 'autistic spectrum' (also known as 'pervasive developmental disorder') is the term used for a range of disorders affecting the development of social interaction, communication and imagination. This triad of impairments may be due to severe problems in making sense of experiences, especially the complicated, constantly changing social world. This results in a lack of imaginative understanding of other people's thoughts, feelings and needs, and difficulty in acquiring the subtle, unspoken rules of social interaction. Instead of the usual wide range of social interests, those affected have a narrow, repetitive pattern of activities that absorb most or all of their attention.

For further information see www.autism.org.uk.

Andrew

Andrew lives in London with his wife and two young sons. He gave up work to look after his children. His eight-year-old son has Ollier disease.

We have two sons: our eldest son, who is now eight, and our younger son, who is coming up for five.

Our eldest son has a rare bone disease, which mostly affects his legs growing properly and therefore his mobility, but which can also seriously affect the arms and hands. Despite his disability, he attends our local primary school, along with his younger brother. He has no difficulty whatsoever academically – it's just running around and playing sports that are difficult for him, not being able to keep up with the other boys in the playground.

I initially noticed there was something wrong when our son was first trying to walk. His left foot was fine, but his right foot pointed sideways – it just didn't seem right.

We took him to the GP, who was reassuring: he's just double jointed (retro-version), he said, it will sort itself out – but he referred us to a consultant, just in case. We waited for a month for an appointment, and when we phoned to chase things up were told there was an 18-month wait! So back we went to the GP, who referred us to Great Ormond Street; at that stage, they wouldn't see us – perhaps our case didn't seem serious enough.

By now, my attitude was changing, as that of so many other parents. We knew our son needed help, so we went back to our local doctor. This time he was less helpful. But I persisted and we contacted another local hospital; to speed things up I phoned the consultant's secretary directly the same day, pleading for an appointment – and, all credit to her, we were seen the following week.

The consultant checked and X-rayed everything – our son's hips, legs and ankles – and noticed there was something: a curvature on the bottom of the left leg. Ironically, our local consultant discussed our son's case with the professor at Great Ormond Street, and that's where we were referred!

The result was a diagnosis of Ollier disease: a rare bone disease, which, in children, causes the cartilage in the long bones of the legs and arms to grow faster than normal, so the outer layer of the bones becomes thin and fragile and the limbs bow and grow abnormally.

Due to our perseverance, we'd managed to get a diagnosis in eight weeks or so from our first visit to the doctor, but imagine if we'd just sat back and let the system take its course. We could've been waiting for anything over a year.

Our son had great difficulty learning to walk. Because of the curvature of his left leg, his balance was poor, and he fell over every time the ground was the tiniest bit uneven. Even at the age of six, he would fall over if he wasn't concentrating, and preferred us to hold hands with him to help him along.

All the sections of his legs are affected. His thigh bones are different lengths, and so are the lower leg bones (the tibia and fibula), with the left leg more severely curved – at an angle of 28 degrees in fact. He has had two operations, one of which involved taking out one and a half inches of bone, to straighten out the leg.

The period after the operation was a difficult time for us. I had to carry my son upstairs to the toilet or out to the car, or push him in a wheelchair. I managed to do my back in too. It was a nightmare time, partly because the success of the operation wasn't guaranteed, but he's a sticker and he came through with flying colours.

Now, on a day-to-day basis, he doesn't have any medical things to put up with, it's just mobility that's a problem. His walking is laboured: there's no natural rhythm and he takes short steps. Naturally, that tires him out more quickly.

Because it takes so much coordination, he also finds running difficult – and that affects his participation in games. He can't catch up anyone at football, and he can't play tennis – the ball just goes too fast. He can't make sudden movements – say, when trying to catch a ball. And he's small too – he was always along the bottom line in the red book that measures children's development. But he's a happy chap, who enjoys life.

It was hard for my partner, dealing with a rare condition in a foreign country. She moved to England in the January and became pregnant in the March – so she'd barely been here a year when the baby was born. She was new to the country then, and wasn't really confident about getting things done, so it was easier for me to deal with the day-to-day side of things while she went back to work. Added to that, my partner is an analyst in a merchant bank, so her job is more secure and has more regular hours than mine did. I was a recruitment consultant for accountancy firms, and that just wasn't practicable. You had to be constantly available, and with the other pressures on us that just didn't work. We had to tighten our belts.

The new situation – and our son's disability – put a strain on our relationship. And it was difficult for me, being a stay-at-home dad. Toddler groups were awkward in the beginning. You'd turn up, and it'd all be mums, sitting together in a circle, or in a closed group with no guys at all – quite intimidating. But once you get talking to one or two mums, things begin to develop and eventually we got to know some other families, some of whom we still keep in touch with. I started going to a fathers' group run by our local authority as well – but it took a while to get off the ground. The first time we went, we were the only people there, but then we did meet one or two other dads, whose wives/partners worked, but it wasn't open regularly so the group kind of fizzled out.

Gradually, however, we got to know people. We live opposite a large park, so we started chatting to other parents – mainly mums – there, and gradually you get to make friends and things snowball. Over time, with various toddler groups, and swimming and the park, we built up a routine, and I got used to being at home instead of out at work, and now things have settled down, and everything works quite well.

I was devastated the first time it dawned on my son that there was something wrong with his legs. He was three and a half, and I was giving him a bath, and he noticed that one of his legs was curved – and it did look fairly abnormal.

'Daddy,' he said, 'I think there's something wrong with my leg.'

'No no, there isn't,' I replied immediately, being dismissive, without thinking, and naturally wanting to protect him. But then I thought about it, and I talked to others for their opinion, and concluded that that was not the way to deal with it. I waited for another opportunity to come up, which was before his next bath, and we discussed his leg.

I agreed it did seem different, and praised him for pointing it out to me a few days earlier. We acknowledged that one of his legs was curved, and that was why he found it hard to run and play football. We agreed that it was very hard and it wasn't fair, but we talked about another person we knew who couldn't walk at all, and how, as he grew older there would be other things he could do, and not being able to run fast would be less important to him.

It felt awful, not being able to put things right, but I hoped this approach would clarify things for him, for the time being, and gradually we would deal with his condition, step by step.

Because he's very competitive, I decided that we needed to find something physical he could be good at. Because it doesn't depend on balance, we chose swimming. Now his swimming is coming on very well – he's in a club – and it's a small consolation to him that some children can't swim at all!

My advice to other parents would be: try your best. Don't dismiss your child's fears, but try to focus on the things they can do, not the things they can't. We're reminded daily of our son's disability, but we make a conscious effort to try not to allow this to hinder his personality. We don't want him to become withdrawn, or to lack confidence – because if that happens he won't want to try new things, and he'll miss out.

When my son was first diagnosed with Ollier disease we'd never heard of it – unsurprisingly, as there are no more than 200 people at most with the condition in the country. Obviously we wanted all the information we could get, and we also wanted to talk to other people who'd had it, to see how it had affected them, and to get some idea of what the future might hold. My son is likely to need a number of operations on his legs, and possibly his arms and hands, in the future. We also wanted to talk to people about these, to find out what to expect.

There had been a support group in the past, but the coordinator had retired, so we set about reviving it, sending out leaflets, and trying to raise awareness of the condition in the press. For instance, we had a big article in a women's magazine that put us in touch with several people, including a woman in her forties who had Ollier disease, but had never come across anyone with the condition before – so that was quite an emotional experience for her.

Through my partner, we also linked up with the French support group; we attended some seminars in France, where leading consultants talked about the condition and patients related their case histories. It was great, because it gave us a format to go on and we were also able to use some of their information.

Now we're nearly eight years down the line and things have settled down enormously. We've all got used to living with Ollier disease – and apart from his not being able to run too well, it doesn't affect my son's or our day-to-day lives, apart from the odd visit to the consultant.

I still try to boost my son's confidence at every opportunity. At school last year, with some real encouragement, he joined a dance class (even though he really wanted to join the football club) and after the first few weeks he started to enjoy it. They even put on a performance at the local theatre, which, even though he won't admit to, he is really proud of! I also take him to the park whenever I can so that he can chase me at his own pace (and I let him catch me as he is unable to catch anyone else at school).

But, all in all, he's doing very well; he's a happy, confident child, and our worst fears have not been realised so far. He recently learnt to ride a bicycle with very little effort, which I think is remarkable. He last rode the bike with stabilisers over two years ago, and even then it was difficult for him because his legs are short and uneven. So he didn't ride it very often and needed very close supervision, but a few weeks ago we took the stabilisers off and he rode on his own in less than an hour! It just shows you what's possible if you have some belief *and* are persistent.

He's a great little chap, and we always try and look forward to the future with optimism.

About Ollier disease

Ollier disease is a very rare disorder that affects both sexes. It presents either as a lump, or a swelling or deformity of the long bones in early childhood. As the bones are weakened, they may fracture but healing is normal. The severity varies but otherwise the child develops normally. The main complications are the nature of the lump or swelling, the deformity of the affected bone and the shortening of the affected bone.

For further information see www.cafamily.org.uk.

Matthew

Matthew lives in London with his wife and son Joseph, who is nine years old and was diagnosed with autistic spectrum disorder (ASD) when he was two. Joseph has a seven-year-old brother. Matthew gave up work as a teacher to become a full-time carer for Joseph, but has since returned to teaching part time.

When Joseph was born, we were a couple of professional people living in London. His mother, a finance manager, was happy at work, but I, as a school teacher, was overwhelmed with planning, marking, and so on. It was not difficult, then, for 'daddy' to resign from work and become Joseph's main carer full time.

I had no real personal experience of 'fatherhood' to fall back on, not having had a father at home at all myself. My own family life had been shared with my mother and a very calm and kind grandfather, so fatherhood is a very difficult concept for me. I knew what I *didn't* want to be as a parent: I didn't want to carve the meat on Sunday, I didn't want to have 'macho' sons or 'pretty' daughters. I never wanted to be a 'father' or a 'father figure', I always just wanted to be a 'parent', although I do love being called dad and wore my 'I'm a dad' badge with pride when my sons were born. Dad is a good label – informal and friendly – and doesn't carry the same expectations as 'father'.

Joseph was a very healthy and smiley child. He was easy to care for and could be taken anywhere; and he always received positive comments from shoppers, those in cafes and restaurants, and so on. Being looked after by daddy meant that Joseph had few social experiences with his peers (mothers tended to stick together to the – unintended – exclusion of the dads at playgroups, etc.). As a consequence, perhaps, some of Joseph's extended family relatives felt his little delays in life were a result of his lack of social experiences.

When Joseph did meet others of his own age he seemed not to be concerned or interested in them. His mum and I thought Joseph to be 'self-contained'. Although he was of similar build, and still very healthy, Joseph was the last to crawl, walk, and then talk (but then someone has to be last).

At 18 months Joseph had that MMR jab. I had had a conversation with a medic who had assured me of its safety but in the three months after it had been administered Joseph picked up several infections/ailments. One of these resulted in him being taken to hospital in an ambulance and at that point I asked a doctor if his immunity had been compromised by the vaccination. At 21 months he was rushed to hospital again, after clearly displaying several of the classic symptoms of meningitis.

A few weeks later, Joseph became very ill again, with an extreme temperature. At that time we did not know what to do, had no medicine and, because it was Christmas Eve, no way of accessing medical help of any quality.

The lengthy bureaucratic trail to diagnosis began when we took him to the GP because his behaviour had changed for the worse following this frightening Christmas episode. Joseph was referred to the health visitor at the surgery. She visited our home, was concerned at Joseph's significantly delayed communication, and then referred him to a speech therapist. The speech therapist referred him on to a child specialist, who referred him to an early years centre that had contacts with another speech therapist, an educational psychologist, occupational therapist and another child specialist! At this time the professionals did not share their concerns with us. Looking back, Joseph was a classic case. We should have known, and mum did suspect...

The following spring and summer, Joseph gained a brother, and mum and I got married in a most minimalist ceremony with Joseph in attendance. I went back to work at two schools and a library, and marked hundreds of exam papers, while mum had maternity leave. I was outside the everyday family life and the assessment processes. The family, for a while, was completely typical/traditional in terms of its structure: mum at home and dad at work.

Joseph attended the early years centre at two and a half, where he was left in the care of the professionals for three hours twice a week for six weeks. He was in the company of other similar children where he could be watched and played with by a range of child professionals.

Ironically, while at work, I had stumbled across a profile of a typically autistic child. There was a very close match with Joseph so, at the next session at the early years centre, on Monday 4 October 1999, it was decided that mum would ask directly whether autism was to be Joseph's diagnosis. The answer was yes. He was officially diagnosed with ASD two weeks later when all the reports were done and presented. ASD is a good diagnosis. It means so little but includes so much. Clearly, Joseph is autistic but moves in and out like someone with fluctuating memory loss, is both severe *and* mild depending on his understanding, tiredness, hunger, anger, motivation, and so on.

That Monday evening, I came home having attended an interesting course in Great Portland Street. Full of new ideas, I had completely forgotten about my wife's task at 'the centre'. When the news was broken to me in the hall I walked into the front room, sat down and saw Joseph in a different way. His hand-flapping at the TV wasn't a funny little quirk but a symptom. For the first and very nearly the last time, I was extremely upset because my son was autistic. My wife had suspected autism for some time and had tried to discuss it with me, but without much success. For a week or two I was sure that the diagnosis wasn't quite right and that the assumptions on which it was based were, somehow, incorrect. I felt that he was assessed and diagnosed for really being a quiet, but confident, little boy. During my October half-term break I had a chance to meet the professionals at the centre. Once the human/personal side of those observing Joseph was clear, the situation was accepted easily. They were friendly, down to earth and understanding, and they explained and listened.

For those around us, there were many responses to our news, ranging from denial to 'I thought there was something odd.' Some wanted to help, while others shied away. My colleagues at the primary schools never discussed the major issue in my life then but have made many assumptions since. Being a male teacher in a primary school is not an environment where good friendships can be made anyway. I spoke to my head, looking for understanding, not a shoulder to cry on. I wanted her to understand that if times got tough and I could not get to work, or was finding a situation in class difficult – perhaps because I was finding it hard to be around children – I wouldn't want to then have to explain my circumstances. I feel that a male teacher is sometimes employed to be a particular role model and that the head may have seen our discussion as a call for help when she had employed me to be a strong member of staff. In any event, I am glad that such a situation did not arise, as I would not have benefited from any understanding.

Talking about your own circumstances with your mates is boring. I have seen friends glaze over if I talk about my children unless what I happen to say is worth a laugh. My history with friends has always been that I am a bit of a joker and this perception of me must not change in the eyes of my friends as it might change the friendships themselves. One of my friends does ask questions but I feel quizzed, question his motives and become cagey, although this may be as a result of the nature of this particular friendship. At the time of Joseph's diagnosis I would only really have turned to my wife for support as we are quite private people.

With hindsight, the time that followed was difficult for several reasons. As a near full-time worker it was difficult for me to come home from work and face a situation that didn't fit my expectations (Joseph never noticed my arrival and I never got a response, positive or negative). Working in a school with young children made it more difficult still: realising that my son did not greet me and that it was possible that this could be the case for life, meant that it was difficult to begin the school day happily when other parents were getting hugs and kisses, and bye-byes and hellos that I was, for some reason, denied.

Later, I would drive home from work with the ridiculous notion that perhaps today would be the day when Joseph would speak for the first time. Little did I realise that I would have to wait two and half more years – until Joseph was six years old. In truth that day never really arrived and the fact remains that Joseph speaking was such a gradual process that there wasn't a day when we can say he spoke his first words and we celebrated. It was a development.

Looking back, it is perhaps obvious why the parent in full-time work is in a very difficult situation. Being detached from the family for much of the day doesn't allow for the 'worker' to be involved with the *family* workings. For me, I had unreasonable expectations based on a daily detachment from the family. Worst of all, I made comparisons with other, 'normal', children – comparisons based on my work experiences and past encounters with children in my family. In contrast, Joseph's mum, who stayed at home, paced herself with the family, knew the limitations and made adjustments to make a happy day. My wife saw the children at the best part of the day and when she was most refreshed and ready.

For our family, through luck as much as design, we have managed to both have an opportunity to be fully involved and to gain a real understanding of our family's needs. I don't see any differences in our parenting style or approach as resulting from gender, but rather from personality differences, our different work backgrounds and different interests. For example, I take my younger son to football matches, which are male dominated.

Joseph is now nine. He learned to talk before he was seven after learning to nod and shake his head, use Makaton, and say initial sounds for words (e.g. 't' for toilet). As each of these stages was achieved we tried to remember how we had all managed to communicate with Joseph before. Joseph has just begun to use expressive language. One day we will wonder how we managed before this development.

Currently, I work two and a half days in the school I originally left when Joseph was born, and Joseph's mum works three days. We live in the same modest terraced house filled with toys we are scared to dispose of in case they have a use for our boy with development delay.

After all that we have had to go through, it is difficult to say 'I' as we really have shared much of what has happened with regard to Joseph's life. However, despite the fact that I often took Joseph to the hospital and was the contact person, letters would arrive on the doorstep for the next appointment addressed to Joseph's mother. This used to wind me up.

I/we do feel that Joseph is as much developmentally delayed as 'autistic' and that really helps us have realistic expectations. However, he may never reach a comparable development with a teenager. Joseph may always need parental support and to live very close to, or with, us.

Joseph amazes me with his strength. In the days before he could communicate he had to learn Makaton. He had to learn to use the Picture Exchange Communication System. He had to learn to use the lavatory, which, for Joseph, must have been a real challenge. Over a long period, to the age of about five years, Joseph systematically used his knowledge of letters and sounds to teach himself spellings. Once he could speak he confirmed to us that he really could read after all. At the age of four he had to travel on a bus to school daily. He has always seemed to have risen to our expectations even when we, ourselves, have felt we are expecting too much of him. Recently, Joseph began attending an inclusive mainstream school, where he has coped with the huge change very well.

As a family we have managed to change and adapt our lives to accommodate the needs of our boys. Joseph's brother does recognise that he has 'special needs', as that is the term used at his school, but he has never asked what is 'wrong' with Joseph. He shares in many of Joseph's significant moments and, like many other siblings, is very inclusive. In the home Joseph is hardly 'disabled' at all and has full access to everything he needs so long as he is not at risk of danger or ill health. Contrast this with the dangers and occasional prejudice he sometimes comes into contact with outside the door…then, 'disability' kicks in. It occurs, for example, when he is made to wait, which is still a real problem, especially when Joseph cannot comprehend what he is waiting for. This means it is difficult to access health care because of the 'herding' involved. A GP can be as inclusive as possible and make promises, but have you tried explaining a situation to a receptionist? Similar breakdowns occur when the car fails. In these situations Joseph cannot understand and becomes quite upset. His behaviour changes, he stops being the happy boy and causes people to stare.

Our outings require detailed planning, but after years it is second nature for us both (well almost). In order for his brother to have what he needs, we sometimes have to pair off or keep Joseph occupied with a favourite story or toy, or a tasty (always home-made!) sandwich. Of course sometimes it is impossible to plan: we cannot teach doctors and dentists to understand Joseph's needs in the ten minutes we have in their company. Joseph can get fed up with floundering medics, and what starts as a foot X-ray can end up as a scene similar to one from 'When The Marx Brothers met an Octopus'.

Some who are reading this may feel that Joseph is not disabled and indeed we feel, given the difficulties some face in life, that Joseph is fortunate and happy and not disabled at all. I do feel that there are factors in everyone's life that at some time deny us access to quality and services that we are all entitled to, and that barriers to access can disable. We have found that outside our home we face situations where institutions (especially the health service and education) have erected barriers and have attitudes that work against full inclusion. Often, failure to listen, to reflect, to understand, make simple needs a problem and, for many, an issue. Non-compliant child or inexperienced professional? Child with learning difficulty or professional with a teaching problem?

If I were to give advice to other fathers, I would say that it is important to see your child's development, albeit in a different way and at a different pace, as a positive thing. I would also suggest that they think about changing the family parameters so that the chid is included and secure at home.

The future is unsure. We don't know the effect moving home would have on Joseph. What will happen if Joseph's parents cannot be there for him? What if one of his parents becomes a dependant?

Our futures require good health. We hope that when we need it in later years we can access it more easily than Joseph can. We never lose any sleep about it, though, as we're always too tired.

About autism

The 'autistic spectrum' (also known as 'pervasive developmental disorder') is the term used for a range of disorders affecting the development of social interaction, communication and imagination. This triad of impairments may be due to severe problems in making sense of experiences, especially the complicated, constantly changing social world. This results in a lack of imaginative understanding of other people's thoughts, feelings and needs, and difficulty in acquiring the subtle, unspoken rules of social interaction. Instead of the usual wide range of social interests, those affected have a narrow, repetitive pattern of activities that absorb most or all of their attention.

For further information see www.autism.org.uk.

Kevin

Kevin is 41 and lives in the north-east of England. He has five children, the youngest of whom, Jordan, is nine and has congenital muscular dystrophy. Kevin gave up work to care for Jordan full time when he was diagnosed.

I separated from Jordan's mum some time ago. I've been caring for Jordan right from the start. I packed up work straight away, as soon as he was diagnosed. He lives with me. He's a very brave boy, and it's a privilege to look after him.

Jordan's condition basically means there's something called merosin missing from his system. His is a rare type; it can be life-threatening, but it's not a terminal illness, so hopefully we'll have him for a very long time. Merosin normally stitches and repairs torn muscles but he has no merosin in his muscles whatsoever; every time he twists and turns or pulls a muscle, he gets tears, and as he gets older even weight can tear the muscle. He doesn't get pain because he doesn't use the muscle, he just gets tears that won't repair.

He doesn't walk, and he never will. He has a wheelchair. He's a very good driver – I've been told he's the youngest boy ever to be provided with an electric wheelchair. We had him assessed when he was very young, and he's fantastic – really, really clever.

Even when his mum was giving birth, I knew something was wrong. His heart rate was dropping and it was taking far too long. Things weren't right, and then when he was actually born and lying in my arms, he was just like dead, all floppy. He never moved, hardly breathing. From day one, illnesses, colds and bugs have been the big problem. Every time you took him out in the fresh air he'd catch something, and there'd be sickness and vomiting, so I knew from the start; although they kept trying to say to me he's a lazy baby – 'Oh he's lazy, he's lazy.'

We saw some professionals who thought he had a mental problem. I didn't think so, but they insist on investigating these lines and it turned out he had a muscle problem, not a mental problem.

He was ten months when he was diagnosed. It took a long time to find the diagnosis, with encouragement from friends and professionals saying, 'Come on, you need to get this kid sorted out – there's something seriously wrong.'

The problem with diagnosis was that they kept on going down the wrong route. They had to do a biopsy, cutting his leg and taking away some tissue to test that. He was in and out of hospital from day one. There wasn't a week went by that we weren't in hospital. Every day there'd be something wrong, something would happen and it was also very hard running between hospital and home, trying to keep the rest of the kids happy and feeding them. It was like living in two worlds.

It was absolutely devastating when we got Jordan's diagnosis. I cried and cried and cried; I couldn't even sleep, thinking about what to do next. Although I was very positive when they actually told us in the hospital that Jordan may never walk or, if he did, he'd damage his muscles that much he'd never walk again; I just said, what's the next step, what do I do now? We got some information and just got ourselves away, then sat in the car and cried our eyes out, because we hadn't a clue what was going on – we didn't think it was going to be this bad. They just gave us a leaflet from the Internet, and said go away and read it and tell us what you think. It was terrible.

Having a boy so unwell, it was his illness that made us get over the shock – because there was always something happening. We were always in and out of the hospital – always planning ahead what appointments we'd got and how we could make things better. And obviously our housing had to change; we had to move house. So keeping busy stopped the depression and the worrying.

Unfortunately, Jordan's mum is a funny character and has some problems. Jordan has a nasal gastric tube and we were trained to use it when he was very young, so we could go home and didn't have to sit in hospital all the time. One of my neighbours said his mum used to run in and say, 'Quick, quick, quick, his tube's come out – put it back in for me,' and things like that. Mum couldn't cope and not using his equipment properly may have made his sickness worse. I got the impression that she loved the attention that came with Jordan being ill – the hospital business – everything about having people to talk to and getting attention.

I gave up work because I knew she wouldn't be able to cope, it was too much. When I was at work I was always being phoned, being told he was back in hospital, so it wasn't working. I was a hackney carriage driver in town – driving round like a maniac trying to make a living and pay for the bairn. I was over the moon. I didn't like the job anyway, although it was good money, but I just needed that shove to get out of the game.

Since giving up work, I have taken the opportunity to pursue some further education. We were told Jordan was never going to walk, he was going to be very weak, so we knew that computing and IT were going to be the sort of thing I could teach him. I got a PC and I've been doing everything from the basics to A levels and advanced courses in IT. I've just recently finished an access to university course, although I'm not going to university – I've decided that I'm now going to go back to work, I hope. I'm in the process of writing a book as well; it's something I've wanted to do for a long time and, now I have the time, I've actually started.

Jordan's at mainstream school full time and they're very good with him, great services and great help, good communication. The staff are fantastic with him; very strict, very forward, and very positive as well, which you need. When he is older, he'll go to a mainstream secondary school – they're busy adapting it. I want him to go to a mainstream school where he belongs, mixing with children of his own age. Unfortunately the first five years of his life he was in and out of hospital with bugs and infections and viruses – you name it he's caught it – so he missed quite a bit of school; he's still a little bit behind but he's coming on in leaps and bounds. He's at school all the time now, he's very rarely off, although he's in hospital right now – he's got a little bit of sickness – he'll just be in for a couple of days and then he'll be back at school.

He has to go into hospital whenever he catches a bug, just to make sure it's nothing life-threatening, because he is still vulnerable, although he's a lot stronger than he used to be. I have open access to the hospital, so I just phone them up and tell them I'm on my way; we're all very good friends. Every time we rang on the ward bell I used to say 'Hi honey, I'm home!'

Before I was a hackney carriage driver I was a contract driver. We were contracted to the big hospitals, and I used to drive the big wheelchair-accessible cars, pick up disabled people and take people into hospital, and I got on really well. It was like I was presented with this child and told, 'You're the one to get on with it,' so I found caring for him fantastic, although very hard at times, never knowing if he was going to recover.

Having a disabled child has changed my view of disability massively. As an example, when a lady got in the back of my cab with a child who was jumping up and down on the seat and was told off, I found myself saying, 'Excuse me, but what if that boy couldn't walk? Let him jump around, it's only a seat, it can be replaced.' That side of things was a big shock to me – I didn't even realise I was saying things like that.

And you have a new way of thinking. You think, 'There should be a ramp there' and 'It doesn't say anything about wheelchairs.' My children say that I've changed so much, I get more emotional now and I get upset easier – 'cos I used to be tough – and I'm more emotionally tied to my children – it's funny.

I just had to get used to all his machinery – for feeding, breathing and driving, etc. At first I was a bit squeamish, especially with him being sick, you're retching yourself, but then you just get used to it and it doesn't bother you at all.

Jordan's so well liked and so well loved and so funny; he's just a fantastic character. He had no chance of survival when he was young, he was so unwell, but he's fought through everything and battled.

We live a couple of miles away from the school and with Jordan having a wheelchair he can't visit his friends from school so that is very difficult. Also, we don't live in a very nice area so he doesn't go out to play, and we can't go out in the back garden because there's aggro and noise and things coming over the top of the fence, so the social side of it – the home side of it – is terrible. We get out and about the whole time, as much as possible, weather permitting of course. We go visiting and have people home and meet up with people, different groups, and we're away most of the summer, away camping, we don't like sitting about.

Jordan manages camping fine, he loves it, all the attention, but I find it very difficult. We have a huge tent I bought, and we've got an adapted car with a lift and clamps and what have you.

Jordan's mum has been away for about three years now. The thing I find now with professionals, that I've had to nip in the bud, is that if Mum's sitting there, they'll go up to her and explain what is happening, although I'm the main carer, so I have had to go up to them and say, 'Excuse me, Mum has no involvement – she sees him a couple of times a week, I'm the main carer, so come and tell me what's going on. I'm the one who's taking him back home, and you're telling Mum everything, so I need to know that you are going to communicate with me.' And that has happened many, many times. I phoned everybody and told them that I was Jordan's carer, so I don't get that any more.

We had to go back to court because his mum wanted more access. I didn't have a problem with that, but I wanted to be certain that the court would ensure that she would care for him properly when he was there.

I met someone the other day who said, 'I think you need a badge, you're fantastic', but I said, 'I think there are some fantastic fathers out there, but most of them are committed to going to work, because of financial issues.' So there are good fathers out there, lots of them, but unfortunately they're stuck at work and they can't do the job, whereas I had an option and the best option was to look after Jordan.

My family love Jordan to bits. They didn't understand the difficulties I was going through with my partner. They knew Jordan was very unwell, but I didn't really tell them all the ins and outs, because it was too depressing and they had their own lives to live, and I didn't ask them any favours, although I could have, and I was managing Jordan fine. My daughters are besotted, they love him to bits, and they'll drop anything to come and help.

I've just lost my father this week. He was in hospital for a week, and he passed away. My mum died eight years ago, just after Jordan was diagnosed, but I can say I'm glad that she went at that time, she had terminal cancer, but knowing about Jordan would have killed her anyway. She would really have suffered through seeing Jordan suffer, and me suffer through Jordan. So grandparents aren't around.

I get a babysitter in once a week, a carer in for four hours, so I can go out for a pint, or go to bingo or whatever – it's not much. Summer holidays he goes into a play scheme once a week for a full day, from 9 to 6, so that's a big help. Although I've been trying to get the social worker to get me an extra day in the holidays, all holidays, so I'm hoping that will come off soon.

He goes to a hospice in the area for 14 nights a year, and social services provide 14 nights a year in a local respite centre. Another place we can go to is a luxury home where you look after the child and the people there look after you: cook for you and feed you – there's an indoor swimming pool and jacuzzi – you know, they've got everything. It's beautiful, it's fantastic and it's a nice break.

I have to take him to hospital every six months for his chest, but then you have wheelchair appointments, physio appointments, etc. – so it's a full-time job. The first five years of Jordan's life were hectic – really, really bad – he was in and out of hospital, and we discovered he was swallowing his saliva and aspirating his food so he had an operation called a fundoplication to stop all that happening. They also put in a tube that goes into his stomach and I've got a special machine that feeds him – I set it up overnight. There's always machines and deliveries and milk and medicine!

Because of my mental attitude, I won't let anyone push me around. I get what he needs. With this fundoplication, they said he did need it, and then they said he didn't, without letting me know, so I had a big bust-up with the doctor and I had him in front of his boss. They nearly apologised and then they changed their minds and said, all right, we'll give him the operation. Since the operation – it was a major, major operation – he's been fantastic – it was just what he needed.

They listen to me now, because they know me – if I'm in doubt I ask them if we can try this, that or the other, and they can say yes or no, but at least I've asked the question. Over the years you learn, and they try the same tricks to get you out of hospital, and that's not what's best for Jordan – we need him watched and monitored. If I leave him in the hospital he plays his PlayStation or watches television, and I'm back the next morning to make sure everything is going all right.

What's kept me going is that he pulls through every time we nearly lose him. I see him still breathing and I know that things are going to be all right again. My positive attitude's helped, and people say Jordan's the way he is because of me: he picks up on my attitude – stop your whinge-ing and moaning and get on with it. I was brought up that way so I pass it on to my kids, and even when he's unwell he'll still give you a smile and a laugh and a joke.

He enjoys football. He can't walk, run or crawl, but you buy these little football characters and he sits on the floor and plays passing, and he'll flick the ball around.

He's got some movement – he's got total control, he's just not strong. His legs are now too stiff to walk. He's got a walking frame I can strap him into and he can waddle about in that, but not very far, it's too tiring. He has oxygen at night, and that makes him a lot stronger, it helps him breathe through the night, so he wakes up full of energy and raring to go.

My advice to professionals dealing with dads is don't lie to them, don't mess them around, because the job's hard enough as it is. They do try to hurry things along – I don't know if they're under pressure to get you out of the bed, or out of the hospital as soon as possible – but when the bairns are disabled it takes a lot longer for them to recover, and they don't always realise it.

I don't have many friends, I haven't got time for friends. I have a partner I see every now and then. I have very little social life. I've just buried my dad this week, and I've been to the social club I used to go to, and it's, 'Where've you been hiding all these years?' It's like, 'We miss you' sort of thing, but I'm like, 'Look, I've got a job to do.' One: I can't afford to go out. Two: I haven't got the time, and I haven't got the babysitters. The little time I have got, I spend it with the family – I go round and see them. I had a huge amount of friends, but they just dropped off one by one, because I don't have the time to phone them or keep in contact. The bairn comes first – not my friends – until he's capable of looking after himself, which I don't think he ever will be, but we'll see.

My advice to fathers who find out their child is disabled is: enjoy it – enjoy it mate. For the first bit, you've just got to think positive and keep your head clear, and try not to take advice from too many people, because a lot of people will try to advise you and they don't know what they're talking about. I took advice from a lot of experienced parents, but not experienced parents with disabled children, and that doesn't work. Even parents *with* disabled children…we went to see parents of a child with the same condition as Jordan, but he was three years older and had more merosin; he suffered in a different way, although they had the same ailment, so it wasn't really comparable. They were just as green as me – so I think you have to find your own way.

It's good to meet other parents and we all find the same: it's so difficult to get what you want in the disabled world. It's all fight, fight, fight.

If you don't use and contact the right people, then no one will tell you. The social worker came along and said to me, 'Right, what do you want, Kevin?' I went, 'What do you mean? I thought you were here to help me. I haven't got a clue. I thought you were social services and you knew what was out there, and you knew the sort of things that we need.' It was just so silly.

It's an absolute privilege being a father, but it has its downfalls, being a single parent of a disabled child. Being mum and dad at once, it's very, very tiring and sometimes your patience isn't there, and you have to find them something to do while you have a break. You can't give them attention 24 hours a day. Jordan has a PlayStation and he has the Internet, although I only allow him an hour a day on it, he just loves messing about on machines – so I give him something to get on with, and go and do a couple of jobs, and then come back.

Before Jordan was diagnosed I was a working dad who liked to go to the pub after work, see my kids at the weekend, play a bit of football and go back to work the next week – I'd rarely see them because I was on the night shift most of the time. Now I wouldn't change my job for the world.

About congenital muscular dystrophy

Congenital muscular dystrophies are a heterogeneous group of disorders that show at birth or within the first six months of life. Symptoms include floppiness, poor head control, muscle weakness and contractures (tightness) in the limbs. These symptoms are not specific to congenital muscular dystrophy, and a blood test, muscle biopsy and, often, a brain scan would be performed to make an accurate diagnosis.

Most of the children affected by congenital muscular dystrophy have only weakness of the muscles; in some instances learning difficulties, epilepsy and abnormality of the eye can be present. In these latter cases, the learning difficulties may be subtle, moderate or severe but are not progressive.

For further information see www.muscular-dystrophy.org.

Nigel

Nigel lives in the Home Counties with his wife and family. His ten-year-old son, Matthew, is affected by Peters anomaly.

I want to tell you my experience of what it meant to have my first son, Matthew, diagnosed at birth as being blind and later discovering he had profound learning difficulties. I want to recount this from the perspective of a dad who also attends church regularly and how this impacted upon my view of the Church.

I suppose it was my fault to ever believe that an institution, even one as established as the Church, would be able to provide the support and encouragement you need when your first child is born with a disability. But I did. Why shouldn't I believe that? Surely the very thing the Church represents is a community of believers. The point I began to recognise is that an organisation is not a living, breathing entity but consists of the individual members of which it is made.

The first person at our bedside was our pastor and there was something especially comforting to have someone you look up to beside you. Even though he didn't say much at the time, his very presence, calm and comforting, took some of the sting from the shock. Living as we did then in Eastbourne, we were rather remote from family so the church family in the form of the pastor was the first on the scene. I still remember being slightly embarrassed by the fact that I was at the edge of the bed looking at my son, who had been born blind, and I couldn't help crying. Crying over what I didn't know and couldn't control, crying over the fact that

Matthew wouldn't be able to play rugby like his dad, crying for the world he would have to face, and crying because he couldn't see my face.

How does Christianity help a dad in such situations, how does it cut through the pain? It doesn't immediately; hours and days later you are still numb and disbelieving, slightly hoping that if you pray hard enough, when you wake up it will have been a dream or a miracle will have been performed.

I never lost my faith – it has been a part of me for so long I would have to lose part of myself – but I did continually ask the question 'Why me?' I don't ask it as often now but it sometimes resurfaces when I see other mainstream children, or see people looking and staring. In fact, my faith has been strengthened by having to ask that question and being reminded of the story of Job, who also asked the same question and never got an answer. I'm not sure whether it is good or not, but faith conditions you to become stoical, and reminds you that others are often far worse off than you (orphans of the 2004 Indian Ocean tsunami, child casualties in Iraq, or victims of poverty and hunger in Africa, for example).

But, slowly and gradually, the recognition that so many people love your son and are praying for him brings you back to the reality of life. When the prayers are finished life continues, and for my wife and me it has led us to look at the Church as consisting of individual members – themselves not knowing what to say to us in such circumstances and us trying to help them. We now spend some of our weekends going to various churches helping parents with children with disabilities and special needs to recognise that it's not their fault, it's all right to grieve, and giving practical advice on how members can communicate effectively and sympathetically with each other.

There were many occasions when members looked at you as if you were a bad parent because your child was making a noise in church. Part of the education process is about people trying first to understand, and then asking the relevant questions in such a manner that the parents can see they really have an interest and want to understand and share their worldview.

The issue of healing and faith was also raised and talked about in a way that made you feel your faith was not strong enough. I think people also had to understand that the reason why they were so ignorant of these issues was that others had anticipated these reactions and often never brought their family member who had a disability out to church. The strange paradox of this is that many church people do not get much exposure to disability issues and assume that such things never happen to 'good Christians'.

Having the opportunity to share our experiences with other church members in this way acts as a positive outlet for what could have been seen to be a disappointment. The disability workshops presented to the church members have been extremely useful; to begin to see pockets of acceptance and change, and know that your son was the catalyst, is in part comforting.

As life goes on, the question of 'Why did it happen?' tends to fade and the questions of 'How will Matthew cope, will I cope, will he learn?' take over. The ultimate dream (or from faith, a coming reality) is the hope that the Bible talks about: a new heaven and earth where the blind will see and the lame will walk – this for the Christian is very comforting.

About Peters anomaly

Peters anomaly is a developmental error of early pregnancy that affects one or both eyes.

Most cases occur sporadically with no other members of the family having an associated ocular abnormality, but it can be in-herited. Peters anomaly is not a single disorder and can be the re-sult of an error in one or more genes, or possibly due to environmental influences on the developing eye. Errors (muta-tions) in several different genes have been found in individuals with Peters anomaly.

In one study, 60 per cent of individuals with Peters anomaly of the eye had abnormalities of other organs, in particular the heart or central nervous system; 20 per cent of cases also had de-velopmental delay.

For further information see www.cafamily.org.uk.

Yuri

Yuri is originally from the Soviet Union. He came to Britain with his family as an asylum seeker, to start a new life. His ten-year-old son, Boris, has global developmental delay.

I was born in 1971 in Skadovsk City in Ukraine, Soviet Union. In 1993, after I completed my military service, I married and, three years later, our son Boris was born. The following year we moved to the Crimea with the intention of meeting up with my wife's extended family and other Jewish people. We had experienced some difficulty within our own community after the collapse of the Soviet Union and following the death of my parents. At that time there was widespread discrimination against Jewish people.

In 1999, we emigrated to Israel for a new life in a new country with a new language. Boris started nursery and because he wasn't circumcised he was bullied; we were constantly asked by staff why he was not circumcised. My wife also had difficulty within the community as she has blonde hair, which is considered to be the colour of prostitutes' hair in Israel. The police refused to become involved as we spoke no Hebrew. One day, after considerable verbal abuse in the street, my wife had a stone thrown at her head, which caused a great deal of bleeding and led to a spell in hospital. I bought tickets for the UK and my family fled.

On arrival, we registered as asylum seekers. In Ukraine, our family was negatively classified as Jewish. In Israel, our family was negatively classified as Russian. The pressures of family life have taken their toll and in 2003 we divorced. We share joint custody of Boris and he spends a great deal of time with me. I am qualified in sports massage and am a fitness instructor, and I now speak five languages. As yet, I am not allowed to work in the UK.

Since we have lived in the UK over the last six years, we have nothing but praise for the support we have received for Boris. Boris is in special needs education provision, which would not be available to him in Ukraine or in Israel. I feel contempt for the system for educating disabled children in Ukraine. Boris would not have been educated appropriately; he would have been isolated and discriminated against further as a Jew. It is one of the reasons we left Ukraine.

We first became aware that Boris had no language when he was two, and sought advice from our doctor. We were just told that boys spoke later than girls and, having no other children, we accepted the doctor's advice initially. When Boris was three and we moved to Israel, we became aware that he was the only child who wasn't speaking. However, the Israelis did not pick up Boris's language delay as he spoke no Hebrew.

The long hours that I worked and the constant stress our family was under made it difficult to find appropriate support for Boris and for my wife. However, I do feel that moving to Israel served a purpose, as it meant we were able to leave Ukraine quickly, as we are Jewish. To emigrate to Germany, for instance, would have taken a longer time.

On arrival in the UK, we spent one month in London in an asylum seekers' hostel. We were then relocated to a local authority flat in Byker, Newcastle upon Tyne, where we are now registered as resident. Every month, I have to attend a Home Office immigration centre to sign in. I would very much like to work.

The absence of formal paperwork and the complexity of the UK education system meant that my son was unable to start school immediately. When he did, it soon became apparent that he struggled to fit in, which was initially put down to his many moves. We were soon visiting many doctors, having many meetings, and Boris was undertaking lots of tests. At that time, we spoke very little English so there was always an interpreter present, which made the process lengthy.

Eventually Boris was assessed and a place was found for him in a special needs school, which he attended for two years before he was moved to another special school, which I consider to offer the best provision possible for my son. Boris still has no clear diagnosis, though we seek all the help we can get.

Although my wife and I are now divorced, we still have the best interests of our son as our central focus. We attend all Boris's appointments together and regularly discuss the future. We both now speak English fluently.

My wife is currently under threat of deportation to Israel having failed her appeal to stay in this country. She would have to take Boris with her if she were deported. Boris is able to comprehend English and no other language, although his spoken English is still immature. His current diagnosis is global developmental delay and it would be unlikely that he would be given the same support in Israel. After years of disruption, his home and school is in Newcastle.

I find the prospect of losing my son highly distressing. I would not want to be separated from Boris. However, I would be arrested as a deserter if I returned to Israel as I should have carried out military service. I feel that I have all the usual challenges of bringing up a child with special needs as well as all these other worries about what will happen in the future. It feels as though I am surviving against considerable odds.

About global developmental delay

Developmental disabilities occur in about 5–10 per cent of the population. Global developmental delay is described as occurring when there is a significant delay in two or more developmental areas, such as motor skills, speech and language, or social skills. Developmental delay may have a variety of causes and sometimes the cause is unknown.

For further information see www.mencap.org.uk.

Steve

Steve lives in a village in the north-east of England with his partner, their son, and two stepdaughters from his partner's previous relationship. The elder daughter, Catherine, has moderate learning difficulties and the younger daughter, Millie, is awaiting confirmation that she has attention deficit hyperactivity disorder (ADHD).

Catherine, who is 11, has moderate learning difficulties and it is suspected that she also has arthritis as she is having joint pains, but this is not yet diagnosed. She has behaviour problems as well and when she kicks off everyone has to run as she is almost as tall as me now.

We are currently trying to get Millie, who is nine, diagnosed with ADHD. Catherine has calmed down and got quieter over the adolescent years, but it's Millie's turn now. It's like someone's turned Millie on and she's gone up the wall.

Matthew is a bit saner, but has learnt behaviour from the other two. Right from an early age he thought, 'If I scream and shout I'll get noticed,' so it's just trying to break that habit really, because it's what both Millie and Catherine used to do.

We are now living in our fifth house. We have had to move numerous times because the neighbours became agitated by Catherine's screaming. There were death threats issued at one point because Catherine was kicking and banging the walls, chucking stuff up the walls and screaming and shouting.

The housing officers weren't too interested in what was going on, it's just when the neighbours started complaining, that's when they actually started saying, 'Right, we've had enough, find somewhere else.'

This last house we're in now, we've actually bought it, so we can't be moved on, but the rest of the houses were housing association or council houses. I've spent a lot of money soundproofing the loft where Catherine is now, just to make sure that if she does turn the music up, or if she bangs on the floor, it's not going to shake the house. Being in the loft, there's not many people – neighbours and such – she can actually irritate.

Millie's on the end of the house, in the extension. Two of the walls are external, but the wall between the houses is very, very insulated.

Their problems have caused a lot of problems mentally as well: you know everyone's talking about you and there's nothing you can do about it. Neighbours are just narrow-minded, small villagers – they've been there for all their life and someone new moves in and starts screaming and shouting, it's not very nice.

Unfortunately, I've had to quit work to help my partner look after the two girls. I was working in a computer shop in the local town and it was getting on top of us, so I had to quit that.

My partner is disabled – she has spondylosis, curvature of the lower part of the spine, as well as another condition where her joints sprain easily – so she can't do as much as she'd like to; I've got to sort everything out, basically.

Last year I slipped a disc in my back, and I've got a bilateral disc hernia, so I can't really lift anything now and the kids play on it. I did it trying to repair the house: I was lifting some concrete when we were having a bathroom refitted, and when I was carrying it up the stairs, my back went. It's still hurting now. I'm seeing a neurologist and he's giving it six months; if it's not better then, I'll have to have an operation. But I've told the doctor I can't have the operation because I'll be out of action for six months, and who's going to look after the family then? So I'm going to basically have to carry on as I am. The kids know if I'm in pain or not, and they kick off more, because they know I can't do anything about it.

We phoned social services about the girls, but they just don't want to know. They said that the children aren't disabled enough to need help and won't even offer direct payments for anything. We've had 15 referrals to social services, and they've all come back saying, 'Sorry, we can't help you.' They've just said that we don't qualify for the help. It'd be great to have direct payments from social services; the money would go straight on a cleaner because it is very hard to keep on top of things – we're finding dirty underwear from Catherine stuffed in corners that had been there ages, so you're opening the door and it smells sweaty and unpleasant.

Contact a Family's been great and put us in touch with a lot of people for support, but it's just emotional support and unfortunately it's not the direct support that we need.

Millie and Catherine are my daughters through the courts as my wife used to be married to their dad, and it was when they left their original father that they started going up the wall. I think it was them being in different surroundings. Catherine was around six and Millie was around four when they split up.

That's when we started trying to get help, and it took five years to actually get Catherine's learning difficulties diagnosed – it was very, very hard. We started with the GP and the local family centre, who saw her for three or four years. Then we were referred to proper psychologists and psychiatrists, and they basically said it was because of what her father did, so we were back to square one. They didn't suggest ways of dealing with Catherine's behaviour; they just said, 'Stop it, don't do it,' and Catherine just smiled and thought, 'Yeah right!' And then it was back to the GP, back to the family centre, and then slowly piece it together from there. We were going through the courts at the same time as well. It was a very stressful time. We split up a few times over it. I just couldn't cope.

It was less obvious with Millie at that early age. With her being young you expect some silly behaviour and some messing about, but in recent years it's been getting worse. You can't say anything to her without her jumping off or kicking you. Millie was going to the family centre at the same time as Catherine, and was seeing the same psychologist. She helped calm their minds down, but in terms of at home, Millie would go back up the wall again.

They did give us techniques for dealing with them at home, but my wife was too weak to put them into practice. It was very frustrating because I was trying to keep them in line according to what the psychologist was saying, but she was just too weak to back it up. I would say, 'Go to bed,' and then they would go and see their mum, and she would say, 'OK, just stay up for another ten minutes,' just to keep them quiet. They were playing us against each other all the time, and they still do it.

My wife looks at the small picture, as in 'Millie's quiet now,' but not at what will happen two hours ahead, when she comes back asking for more because you've already given in to her. But it's my idea that if you say no now, she won't come back two hours later, saying you've already given me this, so why can't I have this. But I feel sorry for my wife and I know that it is hard for her after she went through all that grief in her previous marriage.

We are arguing a lot, purely because she gives in quicker than I do, and I normally get the blame for it. It's very frustrating, knowing that I might be right and she goes against that. I just have a different way of wanting to deal with the children's disability.

My son, he knows what he's had in his life up to now – that if he screams and shouts he'll get attention where he shouldn't get it. So we're trying slowly to show him that's not right, but hopefully we'll have him going to the family centre too.

Catherine is at a special needs school and Millie's in a normal primary school, the same as Matthew. I've got to pick them up and drop them off every morning and every night – 53 miles per day, and on Mondays it's 69 because of visits to the family centre. Catherine's school is to the west and Millie's school is to the east. I'll still have to do a lot of miles when they're at secondary school.

Catherine was going to school by taxi as the school offered a taxi service, but the taxi driver was swearing at the kids, and driving excessively fast round corners and stuff, although he denied it. County Hall wouldn't have anything to do with it, so we took her off the taxi as a precaution, because if he has an accident, he'll kill the lot of them. The school says it's not in a position to change the taxi driver, it's down to County Hall, so they're just batting it backwards and forwards.

If the car breaks down then that's it; but it's a 2005 car so, touch wood, it won't break down.

Millie's not too bad at school. Either she's behaving herself or the school's covering up because it's one of those schools that's got high standards, and is basically saying, 'We are perfect.' But when she gets in the car, she's fighting with Matthew, kicking him and hitting him. If someone's upset her in school, she'll wait until she comes home and then she'll take it out on us at home. Matthew messes about more at school, and his work has been troubled. His teacher said he might not be able to concentrate properly. It's because his mind's been up in the air all the time, and he can't sit and focus, because whenever he was doing something, the girls would actually take it off him and play with it themselves, or smash it. He's learnt not to get attached to things.

Catherine's at a secondary school now, and Millie and Matthew will be going to the local secondary school. At the moment they don't qualify for a special needs school, although Millie may possibly – because she's still in the diagnosis stage. With Millie her condition's been progressing more and more – so we said enough is enough about a year and a half ago, and we're still trying to get a diagnosis.

Every week there's an appointment at the family centre, and every week we ask if the report from the school has come through, and every week they're saying, no, not yet. And that report has to go to both the psychologist and the psychiatrist, and then it'll come back down to us with a yes or no. It just takes a long time.

Millie does drama with a private drama group but I don't think it's geared towards disabled children. She's a good reader, so she's been appreciated more than Catherine when she went, and gets bigger parts, but she's getting on the nerves of the person who owns it, by being particular on every detail (for example, he said, 'There's 28 people in this room already'; so Millie stood up and counted every one, and said, 'No, Derek, there's 32' – because he was getting close to deadline on his productions he was very, very stressed).

As far as dads are concerned, usually it's the wife who goes in to see the professional and if she doesn't get anywhere, then I've got to go in and sort things out. Fathers are normally the big guns who have to go in afterwards and try and sort the mess out. For example, Millie needs a thing that will elevate her desk – she can't write at a normal desk and the head teacher at her school gave her a lever arch file to lean against. When we had a parents' evening he said he would buy her this special adaptor for her desk, and that was over a year and a half ago; it's around 20 quid. He said he would provide one for her through the early years, and my wife tried and she got nowhere, so I had to go in and sort it out, but by that time he's already got this picture in his head that he doesn't want to do it – he's one of those headmasters that you can't really talk to, and we're still waiting now.

I've noticed that professionals always talk to the mothers, so you feel a bit left out, and you have to ask your wife questions at a later time. The questions weren't addressed to you, even if they were about you, and it feels very daunting. I go to every appointment with the kids – but they're probably just so used to the mums being there, so a start would be to talk to mums *and* dads when they're there. They're more polite and calmer talking to the mums.

As I said, what could help us would possibly be a cleaner to clean up after them, because it's doing my back in – I can't always bend down to pick up after them. We tidy the front room of a night before we go to bed, and we get up in the morning and there's cups, plates, paper, all over the place. Millie gets up at 6 every morning and she goes to bed at 10. She wakes everyone up as she goes down, and then Matthew wakes up because he hears Millie.

The family centre is looking into getting some medication for Millie – some Ritalin or something like that – to help calm her mind so we can instil values in her, which she hasn't had in her younger days. But that's difficult because we have to see the child psychologist, and the school being the way it is, saying everything's perfect, that's making things take even longer – but it's one of the best schools in the area on attendance and various things, so we're stuck with it.

Having disabled children has changed my life, because I only did my back in through them, through having to buy a house and then having to do it up – and kidproof it – because it was basically a shell when we bought it, and we've spent £25 thou on it so far. I've had to give up work to be at home all the time because my wife couldn't cope.

Having disabled children has opened my eyes to disability itself, because I thought before that disabled people were just wheelchair-bound people, but having children who have mental health problems it does change it around, and you can see that people have got problems other than yourself now. Instead of being narrow minded and thinking it's just people in wheelchairs – there's lots more to it.

I had friends, but now I don't, because if ever a friend came to the house, Millie and Catherine would go up the wall, scream and shout, throw themselves about, keep demanding, kicking each other and fighting, up to the point where my friends just wouldn't come back. It was more for the attention, knowing they can get what they want if someone's there. And if I go out, it's like World War Three in the house.

For time for myself, I saved up enough money to buy a games console, and when they eventually go to sleep, roughly about 10 pm, I put on the headphones and sit and play that for a bit. It's something that helps to take my mind off day-to-day life. My wife puts her MP3 player on and reads a book in the front room to get some time too.

My parents just thought if I was going to do it, I was going to do it (take on the children that is). Sometimes Matthew goes to stay with them for a couple of nights, just to give him a break; my dad's helped us quite a bit just doing the house, and Mum sometimes babysits so we can escape for a couple of hours.

I've got a sister who's training to be a mental health nurse at the moment, but she lives in Nottingham so we don't see much of her – she can't really help, but she understands what's happening. She's done psychology and sociology – and she treats them how they should be treated, with respect but not with kid gloves. She doesn't label them, she treats them all the same, so they don't go off in a huff. I have a brother-in-law in Newcastle and my sister-in-law lives in Oldham, and we see her maybe once every two months or so. I don't know if she really understands what's going on.

I'd say to dads, you need patience, lots of it; and always stand together with your wife, no matter what it is – if you stand together, you'll have someone to back you up every time.

Worrying about money keeps me awake at night. We're over £80,000 in debt now, that's including the mortgage – it just went on the house modifications to make it childproof and soundproof. And it's at least £50 a week in petrol, ferrying the children about, and it's £100 a week in food.

We do qualify for benefits – the children get Disability Living Allowance (DLA) and I've got the Carer's Allowance for Catherine, and income support; and my partner's got her benefits for herself – she gets DLA for herself and Incapacity Benefit. But the money that I get, that's to tend to the family: the fuel bills, food bills and the petrol all come out at £154 a week. So for the future – I see bankruptcy.

About learning disability and ADHD

Learning disability

Learning disability is increasingly referred to as intellectual disability and covers a wide range of intellectual impairments. Generally someone is considered to have a learning disability when they function at a level of intellectual ability that is significantly lower than their chronological age. This is usually considered to be equivalent to having an IQ of 70 or under, and occurs in approximately 2 to 3 per cent of the population. Increased difficulties in acquiring basic independence, self-care and life skills, and increased dependence on others are common.

The cause of learning disability is often undetermined. It may occur in isolation, in association with other disabilities or as part of a recognisable genetic syndrome. Emotional and behavioural difficulties are common in individuals who have a learning disability, for a variety of biological, psychological and social reasons.

For further information see www.mencap.org.uk.

ADHD

Attention deficit hyperactivity disorder (ADHD) is an impairment of either activity or attention control, or both. The problem presents as a child who is always on the go, does not settle to anything, has poor concentration, poor ability to organise activities, or to engage in tedious activities or tasks requiring sustained mental effort, or who cannot stay still and cannot wait for others.

The diagnostic features are:

- inattentiveness – very short attention span, over-frequent changes of activity, extreme distractibility

- overactivity – excessive movements, especially in situations expecting calm, such as the classroom or mealtimes

- impulsiveness – affected person will not wait their turn, acts without thinking, thoughtless rule-breaking.

There are several causes. Twin studies indicate a very strong genetic contribution. Environmental causes include brain damage, intolerance to certain foods, hearing impairment, toxic (including maternal alcoholism and heavy smoking), and infective agents during pregnancy. All these may interact with psychological stress and social problems to create further behavioural and emotional difficulties. There are some specific treatments, including stimulant medication, behaviour therapy, and dietary exclusion approaches in selected cases.

For further information see www.cafamily.org.uk.

Jonathon

Jonathon is bringing up his 13-year-old daughter, Sarah, alone. She has dyspraxia and developmental delay. Jonathon lives in the south-east of England and works in the prison service.

I have a 13-year-old daughter called Sarah who has special needs. She has two conditions. She has dyspraxia, which affects her fine motor skills and coordination – for example, she can't grip bottle tops well enough to open them and she can't coordinate well enough to tie shoelaces. She also has another condition called developmental delay, which means that although she is 13 physically, she has the educational ability of a child somewhat younger: a six-year-old. I work full time at an operational grade in the prison service and her natural mother and I got divorced four years ago. I have been bringing Sarah up single-handed for 11 months now.

We were very lucky with Sarah in that the day after she was born my mother, who is a qualified nurse, came into the hospital and merely made a passing comment. Looking into the cot she said, 'Her right side looks a bit loose.' I didn't think much of it; I didn't have much experience with babies but as Sarah started to develop and was slow to sit up and to crawl, the alarm bells started to ring – for me at least. Her mother had even less experience with babies than I did, so she just took it that it wasn't that important.

I mentioned my fears to our then health visitor, who didn't take it so lightly and got in touch with all the right people, the paediatricians and everybody else. Sarah did not crawl until she was a year old and did not walk until she was nearly two. She didn't start talking properly until she was five and, even now, if she gets excited she talks fast and her words fall on top of one another and you have to slow her back down again. The diagnosis of dyspraxia was first made when she was about three. They later started to realise that on top of that she also had the delay on the social interactions, that was the developmental side, and that she wasn't learning. She can do the things that other children can, but not as well or as fast as they can. That part of the diagnosis was made when she first went to school and it was interlinked.

My personal reaction to it was acceptance, in that I have a disability myself: I am deaf in one ear. When you have children, you take them as they are and it is then your job to deal with it as best as you can. I suppose her mother's reaction was partly because she carried Sarah and gave birth to her. I think she felt somewhat guilty because, although Sarah was perfect, in the sense that she was physically perfect, something had happened during the birth. She got stuck in the birth canal, which possibly caused a minor loss of oxygen – which led to everything else. So she felt somewhat guilty and had a great deal of difficulty, and still does. I wouldn't say that she doesn't love Sarah, she does in her own way, but she couldn't cope with the everyday responsibility of looking after her, or trying to teach her when she can't pick things up quickly. As a result, when we got divorced, her mother suggested that I have custody because I was entering another relationship, and I was more able to cope with the everyday (ha ha!) situations. This new relationship later fell apart.

My family – parents and brothers and sisters – love Sarah as if there was nothing wrong with her, accept her totally, and don't treat her any differently. I am fortunate in having parents who are very patient, but then they had five children of their own! They are very patient and good at teaching people. My father, for example, taught people to fly in the Royal Air Force. My colleagues at work don't know her; they know of her, they know she has learning difficulties. One or two have met her. They are indifferent to it, they are parents themselves and you deal with it.

Are dads treated differently? Yes they are because of this old-fashioned attitude that it's a mother's job to look after the family and it's the father's job to go out to work, and the father doesn't need to know the things that happen when he is out at work. Therefore you can have this 'ignorance void' of a father bringing children up but not knowing everything there is to know about what is happening to their children – not just in the disabled environment but in mainstream school too. Fathers are looked on, not as second-class citizens but as people who are supporters rather than the providers, the doers. That can affect in some respects how a father approaches services. If you don't involve fathers, a lot of them will back off. If they are not going to be involved why should they bother? They will put a roof over the family's heads and provide the money but, other than that, if they are not involved or told what is going on, how can they be involved in their children's upbringing apart from the obvious when they are at home?

This is a fall-down in society to a large extent. It's like the reason our local parents' organisation started the fathers' group was to give fathers the information that they might not otherwise have, so that they were updated on what they could get, so that the mothers and the fathers could then work together. What people are virtually saying is that a father's role is secondary as the mother is there full time and, because the father is only there at the beginning and the end of the day, he doesn't matter as much. Of course he does. In most homes bringing up children is a joint responsibility. If you don't treat parents as equals, if you don't look on it as a partnership, if all you do is inform the mother, you destroy the fabric of the family. I have known it to happen – you end up with fathers who don't want to know their children. When they separate they say, 'Fine, not my problem.' That's it and they don't want to know, which is a tragedy because the children lose out.

Sarah is only now getting to know her natural mother because for a few years, her mother and I did not communicate very well and I had my new partner, and that made it difficult too. Now that relationship is over, her mother and I have started to communicate because she wants to. You have to leave it up to the children, the children must come first. Even if you are two people who hate the sight of each other, who don't want to talk to each other, you have got to make some sort of allowance even if you go to a park and you arrange to meet and you just go off separately and meet up later merely to collect the children. It is paramount that children know both parents because the child needs to know where it comes from, where its roots are. They should know their mother's side of the family. Fortunately I get on with my ex in-laws. In families where you get divorced and don't see each other, the children can miss out on the love of another set of grandparents, and a whole spectrum of one side of their life. My mother is an adopted child and I know nothing, and neither does she, about her family and background. My father's side, I can trace back my ancestors and that is important, it gives the child a sense of belonging. I have a colleague who was put into a children's home and he has no sense of 'Who am I?' He has had to build his own identity. So society does treat fathers differently, and boys and men try to find their identity, especially adopted children. Girls, they can take it or leave it, but men *need* to know because of this attitude of society that the mother is important but the father...he is just there.

Although I have a minor disability myself, looking after a child with disabilities that interfere in everyday life has made me more aware and less likely to moan about my own disability. There are children at the special needs school in electric wheelchairs; going round that school was an education, an eye-opener, and you realise that even your child's disabilities are nothing; there are children worse off still. You start to appreciate that there are lots of things that your child can do.

My niece has just passed seven straight As in her exams, and that hurt. I know that will never happen for Sarah; she will never go to college and never do any of that. But at the same time you know not to look at it like that. The new school will teach her life skills as well as the education side. You start to look; not at what they can't do, but at what they can. Look at what they can do and the other side matters less; accept where they are going to be. One day when I can't cope she will probably go into some sort of care and I don't like the thought of it. But my mother says one day I will have to get a life of my own and Sarah will have her independence and I will have mine, but we don't know what the future holds.

The inclusion of disabled people? Disabled people are still treated as second-class citizens, in pubs, at cinemas, everything. TV still hasn't got on to the fact that you need sign language, and you still get programmes that aren't subtitled so even now you get treated as a second-class citizen. Until we get hold of the fact that all people are still human beings and have the same rights – the right to go to the cinema or whatever – you are going to have this problem.

How will people view Sarah? I will say it – there are times when she can be incredibly embarrassing, because of her immaturity. Although she is 13, I have a six-year-old too, and she behaves like one. She hugs strangers, for example – the junior child comes out. One of the reasons why I stay in this area is because the people round here know her, they have seen her and watched her grow up, they understand her. She is a warm, loving, giving person and these are the good points about her. A friend of mine has a disabled son and two non-disabled children, and he wrote an article and he put in it about how he has seen more love and Christianity in that one child than in the other two. An able-bodied child sees the whole spectrum and the disabled child sees things in black and white, in a more simplistic way. They don't understand other implications.

Having a disabled child has changed me and my life, and my outlook on life. I have had to adapt so as not to end up resenting Sarah and the things that she can't do. If I had kept my old point of view it would have done her no good at all as I would have taken out my resentment of her lack of abilities on her. It has helped me, in a strange way, to accept other people. I am more tolerant of disability and people who aren't as clever or capable as me.

I have always been an easy-going sort of bloke, but until you have a disabled child you are very narrow minded – you see that nothing will go wrong in your life, but from somewhere somebody dumps this baby on you who can't do things. And that child grows up not being able to do things for itself, and the looks we get when I have to tie her shoelaces… Once you have a disabled child you have to change, and your acceptance has to change.

I won't say that I don't resent it, I do. I am incredibly jealous of my brothers and sisters and what their able-bodied children can do. I know when we were up in Northumberland to visit family and I went to see my sister, and her children are very talented, and I said something to my mother about it and she went ballistic, really tore into me, telling me that in her own way Sarah was as good as her cousins. Yes, she was never going to go to university but *so what*? She told me to accept it and accept her as she is and not as I want her to be, because until I did that I was always going to have a problem. It's not the child or parents with the problem, it's society that has a problem. The problem for parents is not accepting their child as they are.

Growing up with my disability, yes, I remember being jealous of what my brothers and sisters could do and achieve what I couldn't. My younger brother and I were left in the home in our late teens while my parents took the younger ones on holiday. My dad said it will make or break them, and we learned so much about each other and we understood that we were jealous of each other – he was jealous of what I was prepared to do and I was jealous of what he could do. That is an acceptance. Learn to accept your child as an individual and don't treat the disabled child differently.

My mother admitted that she was more protective of me and it is difficult. The tendency is to protect, but you can't do that. Sarah will be in the wide world on her own one day and if I overprotect her she will be lost. The tendency is to stop them doing the things they want to do, but you can't. Sarah has little sense of road safety. Like a six-year-old she has no awareness of danger. I could take her into the paedophile wing of the prison and she would hug every man there. The innocence is there, and that makes it difficult.

If my family had changed towards me, if they hadn't accepted Sarah, if they had wanted her locked away and had ostracised her, my reaction would have been different – I would have had to choose my family or my child. But my family accepted her and that is very important. A disabled child is there and you are going to need the support of your wider family as a sounding board, someone who you can pass the child on to for a few hours to give you a break. Sarah goes to both grandparents in the holidays to give me a chance to relax. OK, your grandchild is deaf, blind, whatever – they are still your grandchild and if you don't accept them how the hell are they ever going to learn to accept themselves? How will Sarah accept herself if I can't do it? If I can teach her that it doesn't matter – it's not the disability that matters, it is who you are. The disability is part of you but not all of you. She needs to concentrate on the good side, the things she can do, and if she can do that she will grow up to be a confident, outgoing, caring person, which is all that you can ask, rather than an introverted person who is self-pitying, a person who won't try. Sarah is a trier and that is all you can ask.

People's acceptance of Sarah has helped. It helps if people accept your child. The hardest thing is the other children in our street. Because Sarah was not like them, her mother would not let her out to play as she was scared. That was wrong; if she had let her play, the kids would have grown up with her, and now they don't know her and avoid her. If you have a disabled child you have got to push them into society. It's a breeding ground for resentment otherwise. It is important and it does help if you have people who accept them. My neighbour will take Sarah for a few hours while I pop out, and that really helps.

If people see the person beyond the disability that helps too. It was made clear that I was deaf, not daft, and so people saw behind the mask to the person. Disabled people are still not treated as equals, for example in the job market, and it is wrong. That is one of the things that doesn't help, when people do things because they have to – they have to give you an interview because of equal opportunities, or they feel they have to invite you to a party, or talk to you out of politeness. Things like that don't help. You have to treat them like you treat everybody else. With a child, how you as an adult react to them, and how society reacts, will end up with how that child reacts to society as it grows up. If it grows up with resentment, rejection and indifference then how can we expect disabled people to feel part of society? Steven Hawking is proof that someone who is disabled can be the brainiest person in the country!

What advice would I give to another father? It is paramount that no matter what the child's disability, minor or major, that he love the child because, by his love of the child, the child will learn to love him/herself. Through love comes acceptance. It is not easy because we all want perfect children. But just because your child has a disability it doesn't make them any less of a person. They are who they are for a reason and, anyway, there is no such thing as a perfect person. If you love them and accept them, you give them everything that is important for them to grow up.

What advice would I give to professionals? Remember that the father is as important to the child's development as the mother and therefore should not be left out of anything, no matter how small, to do with the child. Otherwise the father may end up resenting the child and may fail to accept her as a person, which makes it harder in the long term for the child to accept herself as a valued human being in her own right.

About dyspraxia

Dyspraxia is a developmental disorder of organisation and planning of physical movement. The essential feature is the impairment of motor function, which significantly interferes with academic achievement or activities of daily living, and is not due to a general medical condition, such as cerebral palsy or muscular dystrophy. Performance in daily activities that require motor coordination is substantially below that expected given the person's chronological age and general intelligence. This may be manifested in marked delays in achieving the main motor milestones of sitting, crawling and walking, or problems such as difficulty in self-help skills, knocking over or dropping things, poor performance in sport or poor handwriting.

For further information see www.dyspraxiafoundation.org.uk.

Gordon

Gordon is originally from Scotland, but now lives in the north-east of England. He is divorced but sees his children four nights a week. His daughter, Rhiannon, is 14 and has a deletion on chromosome 22, which caused organ malformation and slight learning difficulties.

I was 24 when my daughter was born, and my ex-wife was 19. She had various complications in pregnancy, which kind of gave us warnings that something was there.

We found the NHS to be slightly less than diplomatic on occasion. My ex-wife was told that she had too much fluid in the womb, and basically the consultant blurted out, 'There's a 50/50 chance that something's wrong with the baby.' To tell a woman that in pregnancy is extremely tactless.

So we knew something was up. She nearly lost the baby through bleeding at 26 weeks, and she had to spend a three-month period in a hospital some way from home. We lived in Middlesbrough at the time and the bus to the hospital goes via several estates and takes about an hour, or you could get two buses, which saved time but was more expensive. I was also working at the time and so that was difficult, and it was also emotionally difficult to leave my partner as she was very depressed, worried and bored to tears in hospital.

She made friends with a couple of the staff, but because it was her first kid, she found that the maternity unit was very much like a production line that the midwives just push you through. She found that first-time mothers are treated like they know nothing.

So, for her emotional state, it was extremely troubling. But for me as a father, I felt like an observer. I felt like a spare part basically, and there was nothing much I could do really – and that's a theme that I think was retained throughout. It was like my partner was the one going through it, and I was expected to stand there and wait to pick up the pieces.

As I said, she was three months in the hospital before we had the baby – and then, when we had the baby, she had a 17-hour labour. She was getting tired and Rhiannon was getting tired, and she had to be cut to help the baby out – which was obviously physically quite brutal.

So it was quite a traumatic birth. Then, afterwards, things seemed fine. We thought, 'The baby's here.' Rhiannon was alert when she was born – she wasn't crying, she was looking round to see what was going on, even though she was full of pethidine. After spending time with them, I went home and it was quite a relief.

Then, in the night, I got a call from my partner, absolutely beside herself, to say that Rhiannon had gone grey, and that they'd taken her up to the special care baby unit. I was straight back up there, this time in a taxi. They said that there was a hole in the heart – so we were shell-shocked – we didn't know anything about what that meant, or the consequences. My partner was still in physical pain from having just given birth and dealing with the emotional trauma of having spent three months in hospital.

The next day we had to go to a larger hospital, but because the nurse didn't want to risk my partner haemorrhaging in the ambulance, she had to stay put while I went with the baby. That was hard for both of us, but at least I had the physical proximity and I felt I was being useful – for a change.

The new hospital is a centre for paediatric heart operations – and, after doing lots of tests, they discovered a hole in the septum between the right and left sides of the heart. This meant that blood that wasn't oxygenated was getting through and that needed to be patched up.

The hole wasn't going to close of its own accord and if she didn't have the operation, her life expectancy was going to be 10 or 11 years. She also had kidney problems that were diagnosed at the same time, and she had to go to the other big Newcastle hospital for those.

She had the operation at nine months. They said the critical factor in her heart operation was her weight – the bigger she was, the better the chances of success. For a heart bypass operation in a young baby, the blood flows faster – they stop the heart and pass the blood through a machine. The more mature the blood vessels, the more chance of survival.

So we knew pretty quickly that we were going to have to go through this. My partner was in a bit of a state emotionally, to say the least, so I found myself doing something now: supporting her through postnatal depression. It was a case of grow up quick – there were no two ways about it.

We knew weight was critical, and one of the things we did, to motivate ourselves, was to make a chart, which we still have to this day, where we recorded her feeds. She'd be very tired, and she'd take a little milk, but we knew it was critical. You have to feed little and often. We did shifts and she'd take 20 and then 40 ml, so she got there, but she was always a slow feeder because she'd tire. We'd feed her every four hours. I would do the nights and my partner the days. We had a routine.

On top of that, I was also working as an actor, which was exhausting. I changed my career direction to sales, so I could work four or five hours of an evening, or two to three during the day, and still earn something of a living. I'm fairly good at being a salesman and I've sold everything: double glazing, block paving, furniture – you name it. As sales managers get paid according to your commission, despite me saying, 'Look, I'm only doing this for two to three hours a day', they'd want me to do more – so I would move on. But a good salesman can pick up jobs dead easy.

So I was a salesman, and I was looking after my partner and our daughter. I was immensely stressed at that time. We cut ourselves off from our friends, we were just in this together. I fell out with my family, big time. My own family are from Glasgow, and they're not the most emotionally intelligent people. I was under a lot of pressure and they could understand some of it, but their way of dealing with it wasn't exactly helpful. They couldn't quite grasp that we were dealing with some serious stuff here.

The problem with my family was that my father died when I was quite young and I don't have a good relationship with my stepdad. He was rude to me when I was growing up and now he is the same with my kids. The ultimatum was to my mum: I will not bring them round unless he apologises to me. He's not going to do that, and at the same time I'm not taking my kids round – so that's where we're at. He has his own kids by his first marriage and the difference in welcome… They're invited round for Sunday dinner, but all my mum's kids are invited round for one hour on a Saturday morning. So it had an impact, because the support just wasn't there.

You know, things like friendships and relationships suffered – we just cut ourselves off from so many people. My partner was a fighter, she was doing her bit with Rhiannon, even though she was depressed – and our sole consolation was our daughter. So we got her up to the right weight, and then one Sunday evening in November we got a phone call from the hospital, which said, 'Right, can you bring your daughter in on Tuesday and we'll do the operation.' There was a specific rationale for that, which is that if parents have time to prepare, they get a bit stressed.

I've got nothing but praise for that hospital. To go into an environment where you see children who are going to die and who are going to spend their last time with their parents, whew, that was hard. Then you have to sign a form giving your consent and saying you understand the risks. They also show you a picture of a child in intensive care, on a respirator and with drips so you know what to expect. They really help you prepare.

Our daughter was out of intensive care after one day and home in three with a big scar.

A couple of years went by and she was a bit behind with her milestones. We put some, like speech, down to the operation and the hospital time, as we kept her quite isolated. She had a slight gap in her palate, so she had a slight 'ssshhh' sound to her speech and she was going to speech therapy. One day the speech therapist said, 'Look, I don't want to worry you, but I think you should ask for some genetic testing.'

She said this because of the organ malformation in her heart and with her palate, and because of her milestones. So we got a genetic test – and I remember the geneticist saying, 'If she's got a genetic syndrome, I'll eat my hat,' but sure enough she had one. She has what's called a deletion on chromosome 22.

A deletion on chromosome 22 carries certain signifiers, and the clues were there: the organ malformation – the heart and kidneys; and the slight difficulties with some learning; and the speech palate/cleft palate is quite typical. So it was clear that our daughter had all these things, but to a very much lesser degree than some children, who can have profound disabilities and profound learning difficulties. So, we had some answers – but when we were tested, as her parents, it was 'no', we didn't have the condition. The fact that our daughter had it was a fluke, 1 in 10,000 or whatever.

So, we thought, this impacts in a way. Our daughter's gone to a mainstream school, she's got a network of friends and no obvious disability apart from the scar from the heart operation, but we suddenly had a whole host of stuff to take on board. For instance, there's supposed to be a predisposition to schizophrenia, and we're like, you know, 'F***!' And things like late onset of puberty – she's 14 but she hasn't started menstruating; but that's not excessively late – she's now starting to develop breasts and hips, so we expect that it will happen soon.

If she has a child, that baby has a 50/50 chance of carrying that deletion too, so her question is, does she want genetic screening of her foetus to see if it's carrying? So there are quite strong ethical considerations. As for us, our caring role hasn't finished, we have a watching brief, with things like the schizophrenia – so we have an unknown quantity of care and support we're going to have to give her – that's going to go on into her adulthood. Other people just don't see it; people don't see Rhiannon as a disabled person.

Now she has an average level of achievement. She wants to be a veterinary nurse, and she can achieve that. She loves working with animals. In some senses we've taken a degree of pride in not saying, 'Oh, she's disabled,' and my ex-wife in particular has pushed her to do her best. And I've taken her to work. I started working for Mencap shortly after she'd had her operation, and she's met other people with disabilities – so she has her head round the concept, and she's not afraid of it, but from the point of view of myself as her father, it's a watching brief.

The other consequence was friendships and social relationships. After a while, to be absolutely honest about it, our marriage was finished. The stress and the pressure of it all just really did it in. We were good friends, we were a brilliant team, but we weren't a marriage any more, and we got divorced about four years ago.

Rhiannon lives with her mum, but I see my kids four nights out of seven. My kids stay with me on the weekend, and then Rhiannon stays with me one night in the week, and my son stays on another night. I live half a mile away from them.

In some ways it was the making of us, and we had an amicable divorce because of that. We value our friendship a lot more – and we grew up a lot. Having seen some of the things I've seen, and having to do some of the things I've done, I'm a completely different person to what I was. I was not mature – I was 24, but by the age of 26 I was grown up, as was my partner at 21.

Afterwards we met a lot of people through the children's heart unit fund – all of whose kids have been through heart operations, and that was in some ways cathartic. We had that in common with them, but that was all we had in common, and that was the beginning of realising we couldn't keep living through this and defining ourselves just through our daughter. It helps but it's not you for ever. For us, we were luckier than some. If you have a child with a profound disability, and you're facing a lifetime's care, then perhaps you do need that...

Obviously our experiences did shape us. My ex-wife's qualified as a learning disability nurse; I work in the voluntary sector – starting out in advocacy, especially around disability – and that's not about sitting there and doing what you're told, it's about finding your own answers, expressing yourself – so that helped us in caring for Rhiannon and making relationships with professionals.

Holistically, as you're supposed to think, we decided that disability or being a carer wasn't everything for us. And I suppose it helped Rhiannon, us not pitying her or hampering her every chance we got, because she was then pushed to be normal, and our son coming helped – he's going to be ten this year. He was good for Rhiannon – she was immensely jealous, because she was used to a lot of attention, but they love each other, and that wider network actually brought her on. My ex-wife has now remarried and she has another child – a stepbrother for Rhiannon, who's two; and that's been good for her as well, because she's seen the work involved in being a parent.

When we first found out it was a genetic syndrome, it gave us answers. It was a relief: 'OK, well, we can have a look at this and see what it means.' So we took a practical approach, but we couldn't change it. It makes you ask questions of yourself, such as 'What are we made of?' 'Is it my fault?' But it's just one of those things. We were conscious of things like blame and stigma – but we just tried to be as positive as possible. We've seen kids who are going to die, or with the same genetic syndrome as our daughter but who are profoundly disabled, so to some degree we were going, 'Thank God!'

I think maternity professionals just herd you through the system – especially with first-time mothers; but the second time around my ex-wife was a lot more assertive. We were generally lucky with professionals, though like I say, I was working in advocacy at the time and we took the approach that we would seek to get them on our side.

We were looking for a member of staff we could relate to it. In some places it wasn't a problem, just about everybody you could talk to – the cardiac nurses, the paediatricians and at one hospital, one of the consultant paediatricians gave us his mobile number and said, 'If you've got a problem, just ring me.' So we fostered good relationships with professionals, and we felt that helped, because then we could make our fears and concerns known. So we did this with our son, when he had scans to see if he had the same problem, and the ongoing stuff with our daughter – we learnt how to handle them.

You can be angry and upset and confrontational and they will get defensive – they're just human, some are overly cerebral – but they have pressure, they have a workload; it's about finding the ones that will give you the time.

That also worked with school, because our daughter was on the Special Educational Needs Register; getting the diagnosis gave us easy access to psychologists and actually gave the school more resources for her – it opened doors. It meant she got more support, which in turn meant she attained more and she could stay in mainstream schooling; and more social contacts – it all snowballed – and we weren't afraid to ask for it. It changed us; we weren't prepared to sit back and take second best. We didn't want to do it at the expense of other people, but we didn't want our daughter to miss out.

The friends I had when Rhiannon was born were all quite young and they weren't parents – so we had no point of contact – but what I did find was, when they became parents they got in touch with me, to ask what it was like. My younger brother's daughter was born with fused bones in her skull and she needed an operation to open them up, so he spoke to me.

But now I have a lot of different friends – and they have nothing to do with the experiences I had with my kids and family, because I'm not just that. When they meet my kids, they meet my kids – not my daughter with a disability.

It doesn't affect her day-to-day life excessively – but one of the things about the deletion is that her immune system is not quite as good as other people's, so she's had about an 85 per cent attendance record – as an average. When she's off she tends to be off for three or four days, but the school are aware of that and work with it. So every aspect of her self is in some way slightly affected.

Would I give any advice to other fathers? God that's a tough one, it makes it sound as though I know what I'm doing! Well, I think the more options, power and control you have, and feel you have, over the situation and your child's care and support, the less resentment you will feel. Because you know, if your child is disabled, you will feel resentment at some time. The more control you have and the less passive you feel, the more accepting you will be. So my main advice is gain as much control over the situation as you can, and generally you will deal with it much better.

You know, our backgrounds did affect the way we dealt with things. My Scottish Protestant upbringing tended to be one of you grit your teeth, get on with it: don't get mad, get even – that was our family ethic. Whereas my ex-wife's family was Catholic, and she was a bit more like 'Why?'

But our game plan was always the same – that we wanted our daughter to grow up as normally as possible and we watch, we support. Things like the schizophrenia we certainly will keep a very close eye on and we'll give her all the support she needs. A lot of men aren't encouraged to be emotionally articulate and that's the difficult thing. I've had to learn to be emotionally articulate. That applies to professionals as well, who should also learn to be less blunt and more sensitive.

I do have a residual anger around my daughter's condition that comes out, for instance, if I see a pregnant woman smoking. I can't help thinking that my partner didn't smoke and yet Rhiannon is disabled. Or even if I see people shouting at their children. Above all, I want parents to value their children.

About chromosome disorders

Rare chromosome disorders include extra, missing or rearranged chromosome material. Using the latest technology, it is now possible for smaller and more complex chromosome defects to be identified. The amount of chromosome material duplicated, missing or rearranged can vary a great deal. This means that it may be difficult to identify two people who have exactly the same chromosomal disorder. The clinical problems of those affected can also vary enormously, even when the chromosome diagnoses are similar.

Individually, chromosome disorders are indeed very rare, but collectively they are common. In fact 1 in every 200 babies is born with a rare chromosome disorder, 1 in every 1000 babies having symptoms from birth or early childhood, the rest being affected when they grow up and try to have babies of their own.

For further information see www.rarechromo.org.

Tony

Tony is co-parenting his 16-year-old son, Daniel, after separating from his partner. Daniel has autism. They live in Brighton, on the south coast of England.

Daniel, who is now 16, was the first of four children and we love him dearly. The first hint that something was wrong was when he failed to begin forming words after the age of one. It was not until he was about four that he began to speak. His mother took a long time to accept that something was wrong, but it became increasingly clear that Daniel was different from other children.

We had no shortage of experts – speech and language therapists, psychologists, educationalists – but none was of much help. The psychologist diagnosed Daniel as being 'elective' – a meaningless term, which I understood to mean that Daniel was choosing to act in the way he was: in essence, that he was feigning the symptoms of autism. At my insistence the diagnosis was changed to autism.

Autism is a label that covers a spectrum of disorders. Some children will not speak at all but Daniel, after a delayed start, has learnt to speak; indeed he now has a good vocabulary, though his sentences are short and usually consist of repetitive questions. Autism is believed to be a genetic disorder for which there is no treatment or cure, and it affects four times as many boys as girls.

Daniel was an extremely shy and withdrawn child. When he went to nursery, he stood out, failing to participate in most activities and requiring close supervision. He went on to a mainstream school for three years until it was clear that he was making no progress.

The first step in obtaining help in England is to apply for a Statement of Special Educational Needs. This sets out both the diagnosis and the steps the local authority will take to meet the child's needs. Our Local Education Authority at that time refused to agree to a statement. Daniel's needs were simply not recognised. The day before our appeal to the Education Appeal Tribunal was due to be heard, the council dropped its opposition to the appeal. For months I had been unable to obtain any help with respect to representation or legal advice. The idea that a parent might be entitled to legal aid for such trivial matters as one's child's educational future is guaranteed to send our New Labour government apoplectic.

Having initially refused to agree to a Statement, the council then opposed giving any extra resources, rendering the Statement meaningless. Only the threat of another appeal helped change the minds of the County Hall bureaucrats. Just when we had chosen the school we wanted Daniel to go to, local government reorganisation transferred responsibility for education to a new unitary authority. Unfortunately the change in the political complexion of the council made little difference in terms of provision and help. Even the bureaucrats remained much the same. Obtaining resources was like drawing teeth.

At the age of nine, Daniel went to another school on the south coast. Three years later he was excluded as he was becoming out of control. We commissioned a psychological report on him, which was the basis for our next choice: a charity school. Again we had to pressurise the Local Education Authority into funding Daniel's place.

Daniel settled, with difficulty, into the school, half of whose children were also autistic. But, as he became older, Daniel became more disruptive and out of control. Like most autistic children Daniel has his obsessions and prime amongst them are dustcarts and dustmen! Ever since he was a young child he has been fascinated by them, following them whenever possible. More than once the police have been called out to help find him. I can still recall when he was only four chasing him across Amsterdam as an all-singing all-dancing dustcart came into view!

Daniel is in the middle range of the autistic spectrum. He shares with others on the spectrum an inability to empathise or sympathise with others. Others' feelings are simply not part of his world. Nor has he ever felt the need for friends.

Two years ago my partner and I separated. It was amicable and soon she moved to within half a mile of where I lived. We also have three other children: two boys and a girl. Daniel is the eldest and he continued to live with his mother and siblings. My partner was 21 when we married. I've always been a supporter of feminism, equal rights and sexual liberation (in no particular order!). I never believed in marriage to begin with, but my wife did. I married someone who wanted to stay at home. I insisted she studied so that she could go to college and become a teacher, but instead of going to classes she was absconding to the beach! I married a woman who had more traditional ideas than I did – bringing up children has been her whole life and it has been her choice. Indeed, she resented attempts by me to take any of that responsibility because she saw it as undermining her. It was a traditional family in that sense, but looking back I reflect that as long as you live in a patriarchal society then it is inevitable that childcare will revert to the woman. My take on it is that men and women should share in the bringing up of a family and childcare equally, but as long we live under a capitalist society then that will never be possible. We live in an inherently unequal society and relationships cannot but reflect that.

There was no question that when we separated she would continue to live with the children. Of course she called on me for help but she was the person in charge who made the decisions regarding their future. We both lived our own lives. Daniel and his younger brother, Tom, usually stayed with me once a week and on Sunday I cooked the family dinner. When a child was ill, their mother would ring to get me to take the other children to school.

As a growing teenager it seems that Daniel has changed. From being a shy and withdrawn little boy, he began to regularly attack his teachers – spitting, kicking and even biting. At home he began attacking his mother and destroying things, necessitating him staying with me more and more frequently. By last October he had moved to my house permanently. He was no longer able to spend more than a few hours with his mother without attacking her. Even with me there have been a number of physical attacks, including a cup thrown at me, which broke on my head.

I felt extremely depressed, utterly depressed in fact. I couldn't go out for a drink or have friends round, or indeed engage in anything I used to do. Even the break during the day when school was open was not really a break, not least because I was being called sometimes three to four times a week to remove him for attacking a teacher. I was at my wits' end.

And what made it worse was that when he attacked me I had to use considerable force in order to subdue him and make it impossible for him to continue the attack. I was also worried about the possibility of hurting him when I used Judo holds to defend myself. It was extremely distressing to have to control your own child in this way, but if I hadn't done so then Daniel would be in a home today being sedated with goodness knows what. Coupled with the winter days and nights, I felt at the lowest I've ever felt in my life.

We worked with Daniel's psychiatrist and his psychiatric nurse to find medication that might help Daniel. The first medicine that was tried, Rispiradone, is popularly used to treat autistic children, but it proved of no use with Daniel. However, we struck lucky with Prozac, the 'happy pill', which suggests that Daniel was also suffering from some form of underlying depression.

For the latter part of the spring term his behaviour improved, both in and out of school, to the point where he has now returned to his mother's. Whether this is permanent it is difficult to say, and there are other problems like lack of eating. Also I have to come round daily to administer the medicine but so far, fingers crossed, Daniel has now returned to some form of normality.

Even before Daniel had moved from his mother's, I had written to the council in the summer of 2005 asking for respite care. Unfortunately the relevant committee didn't meet in August and its agenda was too full in September. Not until October did it agree to funding 15 hours a week, and it was only in December that the system was up and running. I had chosen direct payments, which means I become the employer, but the council keeps a close eye on you, swamping you with documentation. As a welfare adviser specialising in employment, I considered that it would be easy to administer. In fact you are swamped by the different forms, including criminal records checks on potential employees. Direct payments are part of the government's choice agenda and in reality are no choice at all. It is the lack of any effective council provision that pushes people towards schemes like direct payments.

In fact the 15 hours was merely notional, because the low wage rates had to be supplemented, holiday pay added and expenses, if your child was being taken out, being included in the overall sum. You'd be lucky to actually have money for more than two-thirds of these hours. It is also difficult finding people who can cope with a violent teenager and carers from the council's Outreach Team insisted on working in pairs.

What I didn't expect, though, was that, having extracted at least some care from the council, they would 'review' it in 12 weeks and try to claw back what they had given. The whole experience of dealing with the various officials, who make you feel that you are privileged to be getting anything at all, is designed to stress and depress parents. It's not enough that you are struggling to keep a child from being taken into care, you also have to fight the authorities as well if you want the most basic of resources.

I have always been a political activist. My main activity today is as an adviser and secretary at my local Unemployed Workers Centre but I'm still involved in issues as varied as asylum seekers, Palestine Solidarity and opposition to the war in Iraq.

Like many on the political left, I got off easy when it came to childcare when we lived together, but that was the arrangement we had reached and it never caused any rancour. When we separated I happily resumed a single lifestyle. It was therefore a shock to be confronted with the prospect of either looking after an increasingly violent teenage boy or having him put into care. I chose the former but I increasingly wonder, if his condition deteriorates again, how long I will be able to cope before I surrender Daniel into care. I am now 52 and as Daniel, who is slightly built, grows stronger I will grow weaker. Daniel is 16 physically, but mentally he is a quarter of that.

Most people look forward to their children growing up and having their own families and careers, and becoming friends. With Daniel there is no such prospect. Yet parents in my situation receive next to no advice or help and are left to struggle on alone. Not once have any of the officials who flit in and out of Daniel's life sat down and talked about what happens when Daniel leaves school. Or what the options might be. It was by accident that I found out that the council has a waiting list for children like Daniel to be looked after in a residential home for one or two nights, thus giving the carer a real break. With only five places for a conurbation of a quarter of a million, it is no surprise that it is oversubscribed.

Respite care of two to three hours allows you, at best, to attend a meeting or go to the gym. Half of the time is spent worrying about whether the carer will be able to cope. There is no comprehensive service provided or offered to parents. There is a patchwork of different voluntary groups but little coherence in provision. There are multi-agency meetings aplenty, but all they seem to result in is more meetings.

Instead of the illusion of choice, there should be a national framework of care for children and adults who suffer from autism and related conditions. At the moment we have no idea what Daniel will do when he leaves school at 19 – that is, if he hasn't been excluded before then.

According to statistics from the American Autistic Society, autism is increasing by between 10 and 17 per cent annually. In Britain it is estimated that 1 per cent (i.e. half a million people) are on the autistic spectrum. No one knows why there is this apparent increase – is it because more people have the condition or because we are better at diagnosing it? Meanwhile we are left to continue as best we can to deal with the temper tantrums and outbursts of our growing children because we cannot contemplate the alternative.

The advice that I would give to other dads whose children are diagnosed with autism is, first, to claim all the benefits you can – for example, Disability Living Allowance and Carer's Allowance – because you're going to need them for all manner of expenses.

Second, don't think of your child as abnormal or a hindrance. Accept that their autism is part of their personality. That is what they are and if you accept it, you will love your child as much as any other children you have.

Last, do make space for yourself, be it by using a carer or babysitter, and do be firm on things like films and videos. Daniel loves Spider-Man, Batman, etc. I gave in a lot in order for peace and quiet but when necessary I would withdraw them when he misbehaved. You have to know when to be firm as well as when to be more liberal. Your child will have obsessions. Indeed the obsession is in itself a form of security and when Daniel is upset or disturbed his obsessions become all the greater. You have to adapt to them as you are unlikely ever to break them.

Each father is different. Being a dad is something that I enjoy immensely and I find that now I am living on my own I am needed more and I enjoy taking time out to cook meals or take the kids out. In theory, men and women should undertake the same roles, but that is not possible in this kind of society, so we have to make do as best we can. Personal change, without institutional and societal change, is in the end meaningless as women's oppression is located in the sexual division of labour that capitalism imposes.

About autism

The 'autistic spectrum' (also known as 'pervasive developmental disorder') is the term used for a range of disorders affecting the development of social interaction, communication and imagination. This triad of impairments may be due to severe problems in making sense of experiences, especially the complicated, constantly changing social world. This results in a lack of imaginative understanding of other people's thoughts, feelings and needs, and difficulty in acquiring the subtle, unspoken rules of social interaction. Instead of the usual wide range of social interests, those affected have a narrow, repetitive pattern of activities that absorb most or all of their attention.

For further information see www.autism.org.uk.

Paul

Paul lives with his partner and works in special needs support. His youngest son is now 17 and has never had a diagnosis.

My son was born into a busy household of mother, father and a delightfully ordered sequence of sister (aged, at his birth, seven), brother (five) and sister (three). He is now 17 years old. You can do the maths of the others' ages yourself.

We had always hoped for this family and had expected that the 'career break' that this would bring would be a small price for the benefit of having a stay-at-home mum for our young children. We hadn't anticipated that the career break would *be* the career, with the fourth child bringing with him, first, a full-time occupation of a continual round of appointments, hospital visits and hospital stays and, second, a complete draining of physical and emotional energy that results in various work being always short-lived for his mum. It has not been possible for her to commit to a job. Always, the effort required to get our son to school – even with the education authority providing transport, to keep him clean, fed, occupied, to meet the needs of others in the family, to hold our adult relationship together, has meant that one of our significant financial costs of caring was the lack of a joint income.

We had received a brief introduction to the world of side rooms and serious-faced medics with the birth of our first son: boys – ever the weaker sex. He had been born with a cyst that significantly limited his breathing and swallowing. Following a rush down the motorway, all lights, sirens and no parents, Great Ormond Street Hospital had soon levered open his rib cage and had the whole benign thing out. I came to loathe the following train journeys, accompanied by these strangers engaged in their trivial daily pursuits. But this isn't the story of my first son; all this did was to provide a brief taste of the wrenching grief that was to become the familiar course some five years later.

It is hard to recall the depths of despair from the distance of 17 years, as this son and I sit together on the settee listening quietly to Cannonball Adderley play his cool jazz. That in itself seems a minor miracle in a journey that has seen some, but has also been one characterised by unremitting hard work and frequent heartache.

Ah, there he goes; the quiet listening stopped, as it so frequently does, after a few minutes. But then he sits again, to play at his electronic keyboard (another amazing development, completely unpredictable from the boy who so struggled for life at the beginning), a source of brief respite from the close attention that he always requires, sometimes seeks and sometimes fights against.

These things are true: how our longing for a son who might run and play football with his dad and brother has changed into a joy that he swings his foot, without falling over, at a stray potato fallen from its basket; how our high hopes that this son might also be an articulate early reader, like his sisters, transformed into delight that he uses his few signs to tell us that it's milk he wants, not water; that the gentleness of spirit that we hope for can occasionally be glimpsed, as he strokes the hair of our infant girl, leaning over her pram, laughing to see the movements of this new stranger's hands.

For us, our son is our continual contradiction, someone who we would never choose to change – even if we could – but someone whose difficulties we would never wish on anyone. This said, there are many behaviours we wish could be different (to name a few, the hair pulling, head banging, scratching – each of self and others; the early mornings, waking at times most of us barely recognise as part of the clock; the complete unawareness of all self-care routines – washing, toileting, dressing – despite now being a full-grown man in all other senses). But these things are how it is and no amount of wishing will make any difference. And perhaps this is what our son has taught us most: that this is our life and this is our family. To be caught up in dreaming dreams about what might have been is a fool's quest, a quest that can stop us finding the joy in small things and the ordinary days.

We have learned to find the foundations of our new normality and begin again to be an ordinary family; where being ordinary is always to draw the curious stare – or was that hostile; where being ordinary is to delight in being able to go to a cafe at all, even when it can mean sitting outside; where being ordinary is to continue in extraordinary circumstances against unimaginable events that make constant and unreasonable demands on a fairly unsupported family.

Many of us who are now living in this shadowy nether world of disability will recognise the story of our child's birth, which signals our 'arrival at the wrong destination', our entry to a new world where we don't speak the language or have the right currency, don't recognise – and don't much like – the day-to-day customs that are around us and, bluntly, we don't want to be there. We had prepared for the world that we lived in and where our parents and their parents had lived for generations past. Our passport to this new world was quickly stamped 'CBU' (special care baby unit), a land populated by strangers with strange names, such as 'paediatric cardiologist', 'clinical geneticist' (just one of those things, no genetics involved, he said), 'endocrinologist' and 'ophthalmologist'. Here, even those with names we knew were 'specialist': specialist health visitor, specialist children's nurse – we knew that all our children were special, but why was it so awful to be told by these professionals that this latest addition to our family was too difficult for us to take home, too complex and severe for us to be considered as able to parent without a vast array of para-parents?

And come they did – about 25 different specialisms represented in that early period. The next months and years saw meetings with and visits by almost countless numbers of these highly skilled, highly trained people. Almost all of these left us with an unspoken message that, while they required many years of training to identify what was wrong with our son, if these defects could not be made normal by surgery, chemistry, additional plastic exoskeletons of splints, braces or other devices, then they had little information about what could be done to help. And sometimes, from this array of (it must be said) hospital staff, the interventions suggested needed to be fought against in order to protect our son from unnecessary interventions ('Please, no more plastic surgery – it will not help how he speaks, he does not speak.' 'But why does he need another blood test? Surely you have the answer to these questions already?').

A diagnosis of this collection of difficulties and wrong things never came. Some would say, 'It reminds me of…' or, 'I've been doing some research into…' and 'Do you mind if we take a photograph? I've a presentation coming up and I think it would be a useful opportunity to ask what others think.'

In the end, I began to offer suggestions to the specialists, only to receive comments such as, 'Oh no, that's just a set of initials, which I don't find particularly useful' and, on one occasion, 'You've been reading into that, have you? Could you tell me about it?' (And, yes, I did provide a photocopy of a journal article to that consultant on our next visit, but forgot to send a later invoice for my own consultancy fees.)

In the end, for us, the search for a diagnosis became of little importance. We know that whatever the diagnosis, almost everyone is different, that the label can close thinking and precondition expectations. While I know that, for some, diagnostic labels are required as magical incantations that open resource doors and otherwise closed clubs, for us he is what he is, truly unique (specialists have told us this, but we didn't need their word to know it).

Despite changes in our society, I am sure that continuing different gender roles and expectations exist. Being a dad to very young children is difficult. In those early months or years, most children seem to turn to mummy for comfort and reassurance before they go to their dad for his style of play and support. Dads can be for the excitement (and danger!) of being thrown in the air and spun around, for the wind in your hair from the seat at the back of the bicycle, and the joggling speed of the shoulder ride.

I think dads look forward to the time when 'baby' becomes 'child' – a child who sits up, a child who lifts their arms to be picked up, a child who begins to recognise that *this* parent is the best baby gym ever!

Maybe my 'family culture' was a high hurdle to overcome. I'd learned that to be a father was to protect and support and to 'mother' was to nurture and care. Some protector I had been, failing to prevent this enormous hurt to my precious wife and child. This helpless, blue-grey baby, with his shaven head, assaulted with lines and drips; this source of grief, source of separation of infant and mother, from brother and sisters – some protector, some father, I had been, unable to make things right or explain things away.

It was a hard journey to learn that being a father was so much more than this, that things can be ordinary even when they are not common, normal, though not the norm. I had a long time in which to re-learn about *how* to be a dad to this little one. For this son, being a dad was more about sharing the nurturing role; less about challenge, more about acceptance; less about looking to the future, more about living in the now. Perhaps how to 'parent' was what I was learning from my son, rather than just how to be a dad.

I learned a lot from his older brother, too. He taught me that no amount of disability was going to stop him getting his little brother doing what little brothers are supposed to do: play football, get wrestled, be tickled, and take the blame! To see the boy first, not all the other stuff that can so easily take the child and leave a condition, a syndrome, a handicap. Through these lessons, I learned I could still have the fun of being a dad as well as a parent.

I don't know if it was from being a father or from being from my father's son that also left me with the poisoned perspective that the measure of someone's worth was their achievement. Not a good position when it's not 'doctor' or 'lawyer' that I hoped for from my second son, but 'to walk' (achieved) or 'to talk' (not achieved – but, hey, it's overrated anyway). His mother had learned at *her* father's knee that just 'being' was enough for love and acceptance – everything else is a bonus. She had such a head start on me: my son's mum, so emotionally intelligent; his dad, so much to learn.

By the time of his birth, I had been working 'in special needs support' for just over three years. I had even begun to read about children who didn't use their vision, hearing, were oversensitive to touch and who had learning difficulties of great severity and complexity. I had no idea that I would then become a parent of a child with such challenges.

While I would never recommend these parenting experiences to anyone, they have made a major – and positive – impact on my professional capacities and sensitivities. I even managed to come back, after a couple of years of this new parenting, and eventually become something of a specialist in this low-incidence area that had taken my interest before my son was born. Now, no longer am I surprised by the intensity of parental emotion or how long-lasting it is – always just beneath the surface, easily triggered in conversation about our disabled children, always capable of wrecking the rational, clear, logical and calm conversation that many of our professionals appear to expect. So, keep both parents in the information loop; don't require one, usually mum, to carry distressing and complex information back home. As a dad, I now know just how important it is for me to attend most of these meetings, as it is sometimes difficult to predict just when the next piece of news is going to come.

Our first glimmer of light came around 18 months after his birth. We had found the courage to agree to another professional joining the crowd, another to tell us of all the things that he does not do, will never do, or of the things that will go wrong in later life as a result of his baby imperfections.

This one was different; she came from 'education' to start with, although what a teacher could teach our son was anyone's guess. She came rattling and jingling into our house with fresh optimism and a new way of looking, not at the things undoable by anyone so disabled, but discovering the things achieved and the abilities to be found when properly enabled. The term 'Portage' was not unfamiliar to me from my professional activities, but it was a relief and a delight to find my wife telling me, 'This Portage scheme, it really works!'

Some professionals recognise that my son is a complete individual and part of a larger group – his family. They provide a supportive service. Some seem to see only a collection of faulty parts. Those who regard him as 'faulty eyes', and so on (maybe he isn't turning to look at the source of your sounds because he doesn't look at anything much at all!), and show few signs of recognising that one difficulty might affect functioning in other areas, provide little effective support and little service to the well-being of the family.

The primary school years were our calmest time. It was a privileged time for us: he ate well, slept without waking and was a generally happy boy. We knew at the time that these were precious years, in a well-equipped special school with experienced and knowledgeable teachers. The process that led to the Special Educational Needs (SEN) Statement that named this oasis of education required our parental contributions to be clear and determined. Were we fortunate that our son's difficulties were particularly complex, including a general acknowledgement that he required specialist 'acoustically and visually friendly' facilities? Perhaps, as this meant that we and the local authority could agree that there were few schools that could do this particular job.

Meanwhile, although our waking days are now 18 to 20 hours long (and, no, this is not a perverse competition to see who has it worse – there are always those who can 'beat' any tale of woe), a helpful combination of his school and his social worker have arranged one night each week sleeping at school. Some years ago there were many special schools that also had sleeping facilities. Over these past years, most have closed their residential facilities, yet in our new 'joined-up services', where we are told that 'Every Child Matters', this combination of education and respite care provides a helpful coordination of services. If only the school wasn't so far away, with so many other secondary schools between us and it.

'Age-appropriateness' – a phrase almost certain to lead to conflict between the professionals and us. Just because he is a teenager, why should he be expected to listen to Radio 1? The rhythms and rhymes, repetitions and simplicity that make nursery rhymes attractive to the 18-month-old child continue to draw my son towards *Spot's Big Nursery Rhyme Book*, and especially the press-button tunes that can play, endlessly play, over and over again. And the words, mostly nonsense or with meanings lost in history, seemed to me preferable to the love songs and innuendo of the modern pop song, as inappropriate to someone who is unlikely ever to be in a romantic relationship as those who should know better would tell us that a nursery rhyme is 'inappropriate to a 15-year-old'.

As a parent, I look for 'developmentally appropriate' experiences as the first indication of the things my son is likely to enjoy. As I write this now, a few weeks before his 17th birthday, he has found an old pushdown 'merry-go-round' that plays lullabies and causes coloured balls to spin round inside the toy. This is letting me write. He is enjoying himself and is actively occupied. What activity appropriate to a 17-year-old boy would keep him similarly occupied quietly on his own? No, don't answer that.

'Behaviour modification' is another of those 'red rag' phrases in our house. There are many behaviours that we would rather he didn't do. Some of these are deeply entrenched and come from his limited understanding, not from 'being naughty'. He enjoys putting on the television, radio, audio and video tape players, and is very pleased with himself to have discovered this. In another part of the house, his favourite programme is 'fast spin', but he will settle for 'rinse'. After much distress – mostly from us – and some broken equipment, our television and other things that flash interesting lights and make interesting sounds are now locked within cupboards and, for the moment, cannot be reached by our resident locksmith. And the washing machine? We now rent.

Trust your instincts. When we allow our experiences to haunt us, we wonder if we could have stopped the additional damage we suspect must have happened in his early months in hospital, before we had learned that 'they' didn't always know best. If one of us had stayed with him ('Go home now, there's nothing more you can do'), then perhaps, instead of receiving the telephone call at 2.30 that morning ('We've moved him from the side ward to special care where we can watch him better; he's no longer grey and floppy; it did take us a long time, but now he's pink and breathing again'), we could have alerted them to his changed breathing immediately? We need to be with our children, especially the ones who don't know we are there, as we may be the only ones who will provide the love and attention that will ensure that others' expertise is available when it is needed.

Do professionals have additional training that enables them to make parents feel ignorant or stupid when they ask what a procedure is or if it is being done properly? Maybe not, but this was part of our daily experience 15 years ago. Be brave and assertive for your child ('But shouldn't you test for stomach acid before you put the feed into the tube? Yes, I know you've done lots of these, but the other nurse said we should always test. Ah, it's not in the stomach, then, and you need to put the tube in again? No, I was only asking'). Surely, the good professional will value the challenge to their thinking; there can be competing theories or thoughts to some approaches; it can sometimes be helpful to the professionals' own thinking when they talk these through to help us, as parents, understand the decisions taken.

We are beginning to find out about what is on offer after school ends. This is another cliff-drop into the unknown. The local colleges offer computing courses for one day a week for local students who have learning difficulties. Connections are failing to be made between the son we have watched grow to the size of a man, while keeping the understanding of an infant, and the needs he has for the end of the year in which he has his 19th birthday. Perhaps they would be better made if the adviser met him before making suggestions about courses and places that can meet his needs.

As our little girl said, 'The others have gone [to university]; isn't it time he went, too?' She's right, of course. But for some he is too able ('He's *not* in a wheelchair?' they ask, incredulous when hearing first of his other needs), while for others he's not able enough ('Oh no, we don't do double incontinence'). I've quickly learned to say these two things early in any telephone conversations with colleges, located in an ever increasing radius from our home. It can make the conversation fairly short.

We have no idea whether he will be with us until one or other of us is no longer here, or whether some sort of independence from each other can be found. Mutual independence seems somehow unlikely, and yet that would be a form of age-appropriateness to be welcomed.

About living without a diagnosis

There is a continuing increase in knowledge about the causes of complex illness or disability in children. Doctors may recognise a pattern in the medical problems, or there may be clues in the child's appearance. In many cases a firm diagnosis can now be reached. There remain, however, children for whom the diagnosis at present is unclear. With the growth of knowledge resulting from human genome mapping data, more tests to identify rare, hitherto unidentified, disorders may become available. Contact with others who have been in a similar position may be very helpful.

For further information see www.undiagnosed.org.uk.

Richard

Richard lives with his wife Philippa in the Midlands. They have three children. Their 19-year-old son, Thomas, has Down's syndrome. Richard took early retirement from teaching in a primary school. Philippa is a dentist.

We live in a very pleasant and affluent area. Our house is on the side of a hill with a lovely view and plenty of space. We have only one child still at home, but he is not really a child any more, as he is 18 and taking his A levels. I had to retire early from teaching on medical grounds and my wife is working full time, so I am a house husband.

My wife works in the community dental service, specialising in working with disabled people and other groups who are very much on the margins of society, which she thoroughly enjoys. She finds it very rewarding and is able to put her skills to good use.

We have three children. Susan, the eldest, is now 21 and away at university. Thomas is 19 and has Down's syndrome, but he is very fit and there are no problems with heart defects at all. He is quite a tall lad, which is unusual for Down's. Finally, there is our younger son, David, who is 18.

We didn't have any prior knowledge of Thomas having Down's when my wife was pregnant. When he was born, my wife looked at him and recognised that he was Down's. She was the first one who realised. And all the professionals around us just disappeared when she said, 'Gosh, he's Down's.' It was very strange the way they all vanished. Then they did give her a separate room on her own and that was how we started off. The specialist came round and confirmed. We had great support after that. The paediatrician was very supportive, a really nice guy. This was a journey we didn't know we would be going on.

Thomas didn't need extra support, there weren't problems with his heart, and so there we were. He was part of the family and that was that. I can only think of two occasions when anything unkind was said to us and they were both in the early days. One was when I went into school; someone said to me, 'You are treating it as a special occasion like you would have if you had a normal child.' And I thought, 'Yes, of course we are, what else would we do?' I found that a bit upsetting. I also had a comment from a relative which was that, 'If that had been us we would have left him behind in the hospital.'

Fortunately my wife's parents were wonderful and had come down to live near us. We didn't know what to expect. My wife had some inkling of what it would be like as there was a Down's child over the road when she was growing up and she got to know him. I didn't even know what Down's was. We didn't feel as though we were exceptional or unusual. We just saw that we had another baby, a different sort of baby. Perhaps it was because we were more mature, being older and marrying later, and we really wanted to have a family.

My wife didn't have to work. I was the breadwinner so she could be very focused on the children. I was a primary school teacher and we had the usual holidays so it was just like any other family to start with – Thomas never had any problems with eating or drinking or anything like that. He was just very slow. So we had three lovely kids in the family. We also had a great health visitor, who was brilliant. It was very hard work but it all worked really well. My wife's parents were there and were so supportive, they could not have done more. We also got involved with the staff of a local support group and life was normal really, there were lots of activities that we could do.

As the years went on, however, Thomas's behaviour became very difficult. It became more like a job of containment when he was eight. He needed someone with him all the time and he became so difficult that carers supplied by social services said, 'We've managed him this time but don't bring him again.' That was a bit much! We had a lot of help from a local support group, my wife's parents, the health visitor, Portage and the school, and all that was good but the thing was that, at eight, it was just at a stage when it was all going to explode.

His behaviour was extremely challenging. At one point we were advised to have a room off the kitchen with a sluice because he soiled himself, with armoured glass in the windows and stable doors so you could look through the top of the door while cooking and rush in and sluice him down. This was containment, it wasn't education, and it was appalling. He was so very difficult to manage that we were advised by the head of the non-residential special school that we might like to consider a residential special school. Thomas needed a 24-hour curriculum, and consistent barriers and structures that would assist him in his development. That tended to be associated with a residential school for children on the autistic spectrum. That's when we persuaded the council to fund him for the residential school he started to attend at the age of eight.

At the one he went to initially, he was one of only two children with Down's there and he began to adopt the behaviours and mannerisms of some of the more difficult autistic spectrum children, so we arranged for him to change schools. The big difference in his behaviour came when he changed school at 11. We are thrilled with the one he is still at now. The head is wonderful and we were so happy that he went there. It is also only 45 minutes from where we live.

He lives there all the time and he comes home for about two weekends a term, although now I am retired I am able to go up there and see him quite a lot and make him my major concern. I go up quite regularly and am now on the advisory council, which I find personally stimulating but also good for Thomas and us all as a family. We have watched Thomas develop tremendously since he first went there. Initially, he still had very difficult behavioural tendencies: he pulled the head teacher to the floor by his tie, which sounds funny but wasn't; his behaviour was inappropriate.

With their 24-hour curriculum and their consistent and constant care we have watched him change into quite a fine young man really, whose behaviour is now more than acceptable. He still has difficulties with things but even in the last year he has improved no end. He can now cope with people. Before, he would be frightened of other people – he was so intellectually impaired he wasn't able to understand what was happening in situations with other people and in those situations he would react by throwing things or causing difficulties. Not so long ago where there was a large crowd of people he would be cowering against a wall. But now he can cope with that type of situation and sometimes even in unfamiliar situations. But he went through a period where he would need three or four male carers (as he usually got on better with men) if he went outside the environment because he would react in a challenging way. It has been really dramatic, the improvement. Thomas has a great personality but he is severely intellectually impaired, and he is probably the least able in the group of students that he is with in his residential special school. The majority of the other pupils don't have Down's but are on the autistic spectrum.

Being the parent of a disabled child has not really changed me. I went through a traumatic time at work, for a variety of reasons, and that caused me to have to give up my job as I was in an impossible position. If anything, Thomas has been a great benefit really, as he has extended my role. At a time when I had a worrying health issue coming up, I was becoming more and more involved with him as I was at home and involved with the school, where I have quite a lot of friends. So for me, in a rather selfish and strange way, Thomas has blessed me greatly with an interest and an activity that I never thought I would get involved in. It gave me an opportunity to exercise my brain and extend myself. Also I get on really well with Thomas, as we all do, and he has a wonderful gift for making you feel special. I look back now and I think, well, I might not have done this or that, but I have done my best for him, and I have been able to support the school, which I have really enjoyed.

I was worried about what would happen when he was 19 but I think we have that resolved now. I went around looking at various institutions because I believe he would respond better in an institution. The model the council wish to push on everyone is one whereby they have supported living in the community and they would use his grants and benefits to pay for this. I understand that this would involve him sharing with someone else with the same degree of disability in a flat, and that wouldn't suit Thomas. The philosophy is that they have a normal life in the community with supportive people around and they can watch TV on a Saturday afternoon if they want, or go out. Someone less disabled than Thomas would probably enjoy that and they would have a lot more independence and a lot more choice. Thomas, on the other hand, it would not suit. He enjoys an institution in which there is a lot of space, a big garden and people about. He needs stimulus brought to him and consistent care. He is not capable of making relevant choices.

He is a very sociable guy and he is used to large groups, so I started looking at colleges, but it soon became clear that college was not appropriate for him as it would be too demanding, both socially and educationally. After a lot of thought we decided to look for institutions that could offer him a long-term care environment. I found a suitable situation with a charity very close to where we live and was very pleased with it. He would be in the middle band of ability and they have a lot going on; various things can be brought in and he is also taken out. This was agreed as suitable by all the professionals who had any degree of care of Thomas, but at the last moment a new social worker came in and said we should be trying this supported living, and when I got through to the head of social services, he agreed. We had to go along the judicial review route to get it back on track, to get the right placement. I went to see my MP; I followed it up; I got hold of the solicitor specialising in public law and I have done all the arguing of the case. It's a shame that we have had to resolve his placement in this way, because we have always had good relationships with social services. In the end the council gave way and agreed the original placement before we had to seek a judicial review.

He's such a nice boy. He hasn't got a nasty thought in his head. People say Down's people are always smiley and happy, and you think 'yuck', but with Thomas, what you see is what you get and he is a really nice chap.

We had it a lot easier than most, I appreciate. We have seen some families really struggling. I think us having the two children on either side of him helped an awful lot.

The concerns I have now are the usual ones, I suppose. What happens when we are gone? We have been very keen to ensure that our other two children don't feel that they have any responsibilities for Thomas at all. For our children, there is no expectation that they will take care of him. But they have only seen the best of him and they have very positive feelings towards him as he has not been a negative influence on their lives. By implication, I guess I would be surprised if they didn't want to have anything to do with him after we are gone.

I always felt in the loop as a father. I think I had a major advantage in that I worked with children, I was a primary school teacher and I am experienced in that field, so that wasn't a big issue with me.

There is an argument that some men find it difficult that their son isn't going to play cricket for England but I've not had that problem. I never achieved any particular status. My father did and look what it achieved for him – I don't think it really achieved anything, so it has not been an issue for me. What I have valued more than anything else is being a family and as life has thrown things at me along the way, it has reinforced that the family has been the major issue in my life. If you put all your eggs in the business or work basket and look only at achieving the best, you are on a hiding to nothing. I do know that a lot of men can get quite embittered by the time they are in their forties because they feel things should have come their way and they haven't. But those things don't really matter at the end of the day, life has taught me that. Maybe I was never that sort of person anyway because if I was I wouldn't have become a primary school teacher!

To other fathers I would say that I think you have to be honest really, in terms of how you feel about it, and not try to be something that you are not. I think you have to take each day as it comes – apart from the obvious things, which are about making sure that you know what the services are and making sure you get all the right support.

About Down's syndrome

Down's syndrome, a chromosomal disorder, occurs when, instead of the normal complement of two copies of chromosome 21 there is a whole or sometimes part of an additional chromosome 21. Chromosome abnormalities give rise to specific physical features. All people with Down's syndrome have a degree of learning disability but the range is enormously wide. There may also be other associated problems, which can include ear and/or eye defects, and an increased propensity for infections and heart defects. About one baby in a thousand is born with Down's syndrome.

For further information see www.downs-syndrome.org.uk.

Mike

Mike lives in London and cared for his adopted son, Keith, until Keith's death at the age of 19.

Keith's story is probably a bit different to many because Keith was adopted, he wasn't a birth child. My wife and I hadn't had children of our own; we decided to adopt and realised it was pretty difficult, if not impossible, to adopt a healthy baby, but felt that if you could adopt a disabled child then that was something we were prepared to do.

I think we both felt we didn't want a child with learning difficulties, because we felt that might be a bit too difficult for us to manage because we didn't have the experience. But we felt that if we adopted a child with physical difficulties then that might be more manageable. I had no previous knowledge of disabled children – I was idealistic and optimistic: it was the right thing to do and it will be all right.

We applied to adopt through an agency that specialised in the adoption of children who are more difficult to place, including children with disabilities. When we were going through the process of being approved for adoption we saw Keith in a publication that advertised children who were available for adoption. He had been put up for adoption when he was two and a half years old.

He had been advertised as a child blind from birth who had been born prematurely, who in other respects was 'normal', but missing some of his milestones. This was put down to a fairly traumatic two or three first years of his life. He'd been with his mother, who was a single parent, deaf and without speech. He was blind so it was obvious there were going to be communication difficulties between mother and child, and they felt that was one of the contributory factors. His mother only kept him until he was about seven months old because she could not cope with him and his older brother. He went into foster care at that time, before being placed for adoption some two years later.

He was put up for adoption publicly and we applied, as did his foster family, so there were two families seeking to adopt this child. They were approved by their own local authority, which gave preference over ourselves, who had been approved by the adoption agency. We looked at other children. However, it became obvious that the placement wasn't working and we were asked, about 12 months later, if we were still interested. At that point we were looking at two other children; we were on the point of agreeing to take another child, but we decided to take Keith and he came to us fairly quickly.

It was only at this point that we actually met him for the first time. One of the areas that is perhaps a difference between mother and father, or certainly between my wife and me, was that my wife was reasonably sure in her mind that there was something else additionally wrong. She thought that either they weren't owning up to it, didn't know about it or were glossing over it. She was much more wary at that stage about taking Keith than I was. I think I had fallen in love with him when I had seen him advertised the first time and I really wanted to adopt Keith. My wife was warier that he was more than he was being advertised as. As a teacher she had a lot of experience of younger children so she felt there was something else wrong.

She was subsequently proved right because he turned out to be autistic, which is not normally commonly diagnosable until about age four. He was just coming up to that age, so he could still just have been missing his milestones. He subsequently turned out to be not only autistic, but seriously epileptic with very challenging behaviour, so he was a difficult child to live with.

But anyway we took him, probably more at my insistence or pressure. I'm not sure if I really want to use those words, but it probably was – it was my desire that we took Keith in the end. I think one of the differences between fathers and mothers is that men, I suspect, tend to be more idealistic, and somewhere buried in the back of your mind is the knowledge for most men that you can still carry on going to work so you don't actually have to feel the major impact of the disruption that a disabled child clearly brings to the family. Mothers are still, whatever changes in society, more conscious that they are likely to have to carry the responsibility and the impact is primarily going to be on them.

My wife took a year's maternity leave for adoption, which her local authority gave her, and actually ended up never going back to work full time. After a couple of years, she managed to go back to doing a couple of days a week and eventually went back to teaching part time, but the whole of the time he was with us, from age four onwards, she never worked full time again. I suppose it was easier for me, wasn't it, as I could carry on working? Who made the biggest sacrifice? She did. I was working for a large public company and they were fine, although having a disabled child later changed my career path altogether. I left the place where I was working and went to work in the voluntary sector, for the leading UK charity working with blind people. I would never have known about Contact a Family, would never have been a trustee or chair of Contact a Family if it hadn't been for that life-changing decision to adopt a child with disabilities.

Many friends and colleagues thought that we were saints for taking this on and some thought we were mad. Others were in the middle and just accepted that this was what we had done and was what we wanted. Keith was a very lovely young child a lot of the time, although he had a lot of difficulties. Some of our friends were unsure how to talk to him and whether to talk to us about him. We both knew that there were some of our friends who did not accept, or know how to deal with him, and we lost friends in the process – people who, after we adopted, ceased to be in our lives. Others became hugely supportive.

We would take Keith to medical appointments and they would often talk to us about him in his presence rather than to him. The better ones didn't and our paediatrician was good at talking to him, but often they didn't talk to him – they ignored him or talked to us as if we had a pet cat or dog in the room. One of the problems with an autistic child is that she or he can be very difficult to take blood for tests. Keith wouldn't cooperate with taking blood – the only time you could do it was when he had a general anaesthetic for something else. He used to have to have general anaesthetic about twice a year for his eyes, to reduce the pain at the back of them. When he had a general anaesthetic, they sometimes took blood for other tests. There were some urine disorders that we were aware of but never quite got enough medical attention to work out what was really going on. The absence of regular or routine monitoring, however, resulted in a total lack of awareness of certain problems, the most severe of which was the malfunctioning of one of his kidneys, which eventually caused his death.

My parents lived in the north-east but moved down to London and bought a house very close to our own, as my father had been ill. They loved Keith and my wife would take him round in the afternoon after school and they spoilt him – they didn't see any difference, he was their only grandchild and even though Keith had hardly any language he had some phrases, like 'Want a crunchy one,' for little crunchy biscuits. He loved to sit with a cup of tea and a crunchy biscuit. I was often at work and so my wife was doing all the caring with my parents and, except at weekends, missed this little ritual that gave him such pleasure.

I have seen other fathers of disabled children who are able to carry on with a working life and who escape a lot of the hardest areas of living with a disabled child that a mother has to put up with. I suspect I'm not the only one who has actually managed to get away without feeling the absolute full impact that a mother and the rest of a family may often feel, although I did try to give my wife a break when I could, by helping Keith with activities that he enjoyed – for example, by taking him trampolining (at which he became very proficient) and swimming every weekend for years and years.

There is a need to demystify disability for men; the assumption is that men don't know how to look after children. I could do the active things that Keith liked to do – although I couldn't swim and Keith actually made me learn to swim. It was something we could do together…together we loved water. It was more difficult for my wife to deal with him as he got older, it was hard for her to take him into the female changing rooms as he got older and he was stronger in the water, so it became something only I could do with him. Maybe some fathers don't feel that they can do with a disabled child what they could do with a non-disabled child. Find what you *can* do, there may be areas of interest that you can share and maybe there is a role for authorities to develop bonding activities for fathers with children.

Keith certainly changed our lives absolutely, totally, dramatically. We went from having no children to having a four-year-old with disabilities that, as the months went on, seemed to become more severe then we had originally thought. He went to special schools throughout his life. One of the areas where life changed for both of us, but probably more for my wife, because she single-mindedly focused on his development, was the extent to which she became a campaigner for what we felt Keith needed in his life. Whether it was type of school, respite care, holiday activities, whether it was good medical care rather than inadequate medical support, benefits – everything that goes with having a disabled child.

I don't know whether fathers are treated differently, but mothers are better known to professionals – although I could take time off from work and make work up at the weekend and in the evening, so I could attend some meetings as well. We did a lot of meetings together. I suspect, though, that there were times when my wife was more assertive with professionals, whereas I was more reserved, more looking for a logical explanation or listening to reasons. She just wanted things to be better and so she tended to be firmer, which was absolutely right for getting things done. Sometimes professionals chose to speak to me as they thought they would be let off easier. On the other hand, she developed a very strong relationship with some professionals, a relationship of mutual respect with those who were clearly interested in helping Keith or cared about us or put themselves out.

Kids in the street were the most hurtful of the lot. Keith didn't walk normally or straight and might sit down in the road, and other kids would look at him and shout rude words at him. That made me want to go up and give them an earful. But, being rational, you should go up to them and say, 'Do you realise he is blind and he can't do the things that you like doing?' Very often kids would realise they had said and done the wrong thing and become conscious of their own mistake in mocking in the first place. But sometimes it wasn't easy to be rational to a child who was being rude. It wasn't just children. Keith was in a buggy a lot of the time and my wife was determined that he would walk and would be firm with him that he would walk. One particular couple saw her looking as if she was being excessively firm with him and approached her in the street very crossly. She explained his background. They didn't know about disability and became very supportive over the years, asking about how he was getting on, and in our local area we became quite well known. I think my wife educated a lot of people about disabled people, about the issues. What emerged out of that was a better understanding for some people.

My experiences have fundamentally changed my views of disabled people – coming from a position where you don't understand these people because you don't live or work with them, to the point where the disability doesn't matter, the person is a person first and has a disability second. The rest of the world often doesn't treat disabled people fairly and you tend to be more vociferous on their behalf. My life changed totally – my attitudes and the importance of striving to provide the right support, the right care and the right benefits. It changes your life – both your day-to-day life in terms of what you can and can't do, but it also changes who you are in terms of awareness and attitude, and the desire to see improvements for disabled people.

Keith stayed in day school until the age of 15, which meant that he was invariably travelling long distances. One thing we fought for and got was for him not to have to go to local special schools, but to go to specialist special schools which were out of the borough. So he went first to a school for blind children in another part of London, he went to a junior school for autistic children in Essex and then, because my wife particularly felt that one of the things he needed most was love and care and not pure education, he went to a school run by a charity for children with cerebral palsy, many of whom have additional difficulties such as sight loss and learning difficulties.

His education had been very much influenced by his blindness; the older he got the less the blindness element influenced the choice of education and the more it became about his wider range of difficulties. If a school could see the whole child and provide for disability more generally in a loving environment, the better it was for Keith.

At 15, there was some difference of opinion between us. I would have been keen to keep him at home longer. My wife wanted to keep him at home longer as well, but she was more acutely aware that as he got bigger it was harder to do that. We agreed to a weekly placement at the same school. So he travelled out Monday morning and came home Friday evening. He came home most weekends. That was not least because it was becoming increasingly difficult to get sufficiently substantial care packages to allow us some respite. One of the problems was that he didn't sleep very well. So it could often be 1 or 2 in the morning before he went to sleep and he might sleep for four or five hours and if he wasn't asleep you weren't sure how safe he was, because he could get out of his room and disappear. Was he going to fall down the stairs? There was no use putting gates on stairs as he was very clever, he knew how to undo things like that. Anyway we had no intention to lock him in his room. One of the differences between us was that my wife often got a lot less sleep as she tended to stay awake until he went to sleep, particularly for my sake as I had to go to work, but in truth, because she worried about him more. Later on, our paediatrician found a medication that helped him sleep, which made life a lot better.

Nonetheless he was still very much a handful and getting care provision was difficult even though we did well compared to most families. This was not least because my wife fought for a decent care package.

Keith was in a weekly placement until he was 18 and then we had huge traumas in finding an adult placement for him. If you think life is tough with a disabled child up until age 18, see what it's like after that, because so many of the services that you had just disappear. You are into adult services and you have lost paediatric support. Education has to be vocational, otherwise it is very hard to find placements and, if you are severely disabled, vocational placements are very difficult to get. The choices were few and the best option was 150 miles from home, not something we wanted.

At 18 Keith went to an adult establishment, a college for people with disabilities, particularly autism and challenging behaviour disorders. Keith's behaviour was quite mild compared to that of a lot of the young people there and at times we felt it was quite inappropriate for him to be with some of the other residents. However, it provided facilities for what he wanted and needed. It gave him the chance to run, climb, swim and have the freedom to move about that was essential. It wasn't all good, but it was the best we could find. The carers there became very fond of him.

Whilst there, he was unsettled and we put it down to change of people, change of routine, change of team and change of surroundings. He started to go off his food having always been a great eater, a big lad, and it became obvious after a while that something was wrong. Being in the adult system, there was no paediatric support and finding adequate medical care was quite difficult, reliant on the best there was in local general hospitals where they're not as experienced in specialist areas. It was a culture shock.

He had only one kidney and that was degenerating. He died of kidney failure at the age of 19. It transpired that, despite all the expert medical help we had had, there were contra-indications with his epilepsy medications for kidney problems. It might have stopped him from having epileptic fits quite so often but, unknown to us, it affected his kidneys.

My wife always felt more capable of spotting things than I was and was often more in tune with the things that were wrong with him. There were times when I did not believe that it was as serious as she did. Of course she was right in the end to be more sceptical of what they were saying. I had less of a tendency to believe things were as bad as they might be – I didn't want to hear it and I did not want to know it as I felt responsible for bringing this child into our family, so the tendency in me was to want to deny some of the emerging evidence.

We did get help from some agencies. We didn't, however, know about Contact a Family, but locally there was a disabled childcare centre; it had faults but it did have a lot of good things going for it, which meant that Keith got services that he would not have had in other boroughs. My wife in particular wanted to praise when we were helped as we often were, but to be able to complain when things were bad – as they were from time to time.

What didn't help was a lack of resources in some areas, and those professionals who would not go the extra mile for you. Did we have any right to expect that they should? The fact that you had to fight for so much rather than that services were there as a right was the added millstone over and above the pressures imposed by your child.

Having services 9 to 5, when men tend to be at work, is not helpful. There is a role for more services and out-of-hours opportunities for both parents to be involved together. Keith went to a clinic for psychotherapy and they ran parent groups in the evening; sometimes I went to that on my own out of work hours.

I still sense that there is some reluctance in fathers to engage. But the fact that this book is being written takes fathers up the agenda and let's not allow a continuation of the view that parenting or caring is almost exclusively a mother's role, particularly in the early years.

Campaigning for paternity leave and carers' leave, and removing disability discrimination has been an important development in society in the last 10 or 20 years. The more paternity leave is seen in the same way as maternity leave and is allowed as a substantial amount of time off, the more fathers will be drawn into early years childcare in particular. Women are not the only gender who care, but in many families it is still assumed that parenting is female led and I suspect that this is exacerbated with disabled children.

What advice would I give to other fathers? I would say to be conscious of and think through the pressure that is put on a mother with a disabled child. Be conscious of the impact on the whole family. Remember that a disabled child isn't going to bite (proverbially at least!). You can share the joint role and responsibility of looking after your child but try to find something you can uniquely do as a father – something that will give you and your child pleasure.

I loved going trampolining and swimming with Keith. It was tiring, it was hard work and sometimes it got a bit repetitive, but I loved the enjoyment that he got out of it and I had a sense of pleasure and pride in knowing that I had been there when he got to Stage 4 trampoline badge because he became good enough to get there. Who had helped him – well coaches had, but I'd been there week in week out with him. So it may be hard but there are pleasures in it too and I will always remember that he taught me to swim. I would not have learnt if he hadn't made me do it, in his own way!

One of the things that is always there is that he died. I wonder, did he have to die and what would it be like if he was still alive? Before we knew he was seriously ill we never knew what adult life would be like for him and especially after we had died. But were there other things that we could have done that could have saved his life? I don't think there was anything else that my wife could have done; I could maybe have worked harder at times, but I don't think there is anything that she could have done, although she will still blame herself for not having done this or that or been aware of something that she feels she should have known about.

She was the most fantastic mother a child could have had. I was not the most fantastic father – I wasn't there because I was working most of the time, although I am aware that I certainly gave more than many fathers would have given because I could get time off when I needed it. But I don't feel I made the contribution to his development that she did. There is still a nagging feeling that I should have done more.

But, more than that, I still feel that there is a lack of rights for disabled people. The fact that many disabled children do not have the same access to education or services as other children, and get fobbed off with second best. You can still be the victim of what is seen to be good, like inclusion in education when there are still some children for whom inclusion is not an advantage. You simply couldn't put Keith in a mainstream class. It is a good idea for those who can be included, but there are some who can't and doctrinaire solutions often don't suit.

Social justice, moving the world forward, is extremely important, but it doesn't look like the same thing for all disabled people. Different people need different services and support. Maybe the world is getting better but there is still a long way to go.

At the end this feels like a series of complaints about inadequate support for disabled children. There are a lot of carers and other professionals who do a great job and more organisations like Contact a Family providing invaluable support. We had a child who was hard work but for both mother and father he was loved and he gave love back – so despite our differences we were one about Keith!

About autism and epilepsy

Autism

The 'autistic spectrum' (also known as 'pervasive developmental disorder') is the term used for a range of disorders affecting the development of social interaction, communication and imagination. This triad of impairments may be due to severe problems in making sense of experiences, especially the complicated, constantly changing social world. This results in a lack of imaginative understanding of other people's thoughts, feelings and needs, and difficulty in acquiring the subtle, unspoken rules of social interaction. Instead of the usual wide range of social interests, those affected have a narrow, repetitive pattern of activities that absorb most or all of their attention.

For further information see www.nas.org.uk.

Epilepsy

Epilepsy is the tendency to have recurrent seizures originating in the brain as a result of excessive or disordered discharge of brain cells. Causes of epilepsy are variable.

For further information see www.epilepsynse.org.uk.

Edward

Edward lives in the south of England with his 19-year-old son who was born with CHARGE association.

My son was born in 1987 with CHARGE association, which meant, in his case, that he was deaf-blind. He also had facial palsy and was generally very weak and floppy. He was rushed to intensive care. When I saw him the next day I immediately realised that there was something seriously wrong, but it took several weeks for the paediatric consultant to confirm that there was any problem and then to identify it.

The cause of some disabilities is known but, when my son was born, the cause of CHARGE was not. It was felt then that the probability was that it was caused by an attack by some damaging substance during the early period of gestation. Only very recently was a genetic cause identified.

The pressure of serious disability is colossal. My wife had a very difficult time in labour. I had made the mistake of engaging a top gynae-cologist, who overruled the instinctive concerns of the midwife. When a baby is rushed away to a baby unit there is no chance of bonding. My wife felt responsible for the disability. As a dad I found the position difficult because my role was to support and do the practical things rather than to howl like a dog. Once our son was allowed home we had to nurse him 24 hours a day. We had to learn a lot, including how to insert a nasal gastric tube and basic physiotherapy to keep his lungs clear. He was at constant risk of stopping breathing. Or, more accurately perhaps, he *appeared* to be at constant risk and our fear was heightened by the

warnings of medical supervisors. I now believe that he was far less likely
to stop breathing than we were advised (now a tracheotomy is often
advised, but I question the wisdom of this). We had a breathing monitor,
which was totally useless. It produced false alarms all the time and you
can imagine the stress of hearing the alarm and rushing to the cot expecting to find the baby dead or dying. Eventually I lost my temper and threw
the alarm against the wall. After that, my wife and I found life easier.

Instinct is often a better guide than medical advice in my personal
view. For example, when our son was five, weighed about 40 lb and
developed viral pneumonia we were called back to the hospital (we had
just got home from a visit) because he was said to be on the brink of
death. When we reached his cot he did look on the verge of death.
Regardless of the complaints of the nurses my wife picked him up,
shedding various life support and monitoring devices. Although very
feeble, he giggled. I knew then that he would live. A parent's embrace was
far more important than medical treatment.

Going back to the early days, we nursed him 24 hours a day in shifts
for about a year. I do not think that we have recovered from the physical
and emotional strain. Outside support was very patchy. We had an excellent
health visitor. She was on the verge of retirement and was one of the old
school, with a lifetime of experience. We found a fantastic cranial osteopath (cranial osteopathy was an anathema in 1987), who did a great deal
of good. When she began treating the facial paralysis, our son, who was
generally inert, immediately raised his hand to touch the spot. After about
a year, we found a marvellous woman in the village who helped in his care
and, being both experienced with children and slightly removed, she was
able to drive him forward. On the other hand, overall medical advice was
vague, confused and often contradictory. There are a number of charities
and other bodies that can provide vital help, information and guidance
but you have to seek them out. We were a professional couple and it still
took us years to find just some of these; *they* should find the parents –
some system enabling comprehensive information on benefits, grants,
practical help, key literature, and so on, to be brought urgently to parents'
attention would not be difficult to devise.

By the time our son was 18 months old he was doing very well. He
was about six months behind an average child. He was beginning to eat
mashed solid foods, to pull himself up on furniture and to speak about 20
words. At this point he developed a hiatus hernia. I now know that hiatus

hernias are recognised as a possible symptom of CHARGE and that his presentation was classic. He was frequently sick, mainly during or after eating. He would sick up blood, especially at night. What had happened is that the valve at the top of his stomach had weakened allowing stomach acids to cause severe and painful ulceration of his oesophagus. The medics, including the consultant paediatrician, failed to diagnose (or openly diagnose) the hernia. For the next three and a half years, we battled to keep him alive. The main task was to force food and liquid into him. He would refuse to eat and twice over the years during tantrums I slapped him (not hard enough to mark him) in my desperation that he should eat. I was guilty then, but felt even worse when I understood the pain that eating had caused him. He stuck at about 40 lb and suffered one infection after another. He was seriously anaemic to the extent that he needed blood transfusions. He shut down all but the most vital life support systems, so that he stopped speaking and has not spoken since. He had grommets fitted in his ears purportedly to ease his ear infections, but now it is my opinion that grommets are an abomination to be avoided at all costs. I say this because it involves a significant operative procedure and this is best avoided if possible in cases of young children who are already in poor health, or who cannot readily understand what is happening and why. Grommets frequently fall out with an, albeit small, risk of damage to the eardrum. They curtail normal living in that there is a strong recommendation to prevent bath water, swimming pool water, and so on, entering the ear and penetrating through the grommet, but bathing and swimming are often major sources of enjoyment and exercise for disabled children. In my son's case, and in many other cases I have come across, the insertion of grommets marked a striking increase in the number and severity of ear infections. Ten years ago grommets were an easy quick-fix solution offered by specialists to trusting parents. Hopefully things have changed.

After about five years we were offered respite care, but after a trial hour he went off for his second respite visit and came back with a broken leg. That put us off.

Of course we asked whether anything could be done and were always told that any steps to alleviate his symptoms would probably kill him. As a parent, life seems all important. Foolishly we believed what we were told. After he recovered miraculously from his pneumonia our consultant, about whom we always had serious doubts, resigned from the NHS and we were assigned a new consultant. She was far better and, having just gone through the pneumonia, I pointed out that he was going to die sooner or later in any event. I demanded an operation regardless of the risk. I was referred to a specialist hospital and that was the turning point. The professor who looked after our son was astonished to hear that there was any risk and said that he did half a dozen of the operations a week and had never lost a patient. He did what was then called a Nissan's fundoplication (tightening up the top of the stomach) and repositioned the gastronomy button so that it was in the correct place. After that our son was like one of those magic paper flowers dropped in water. He bloomed, grew and developed, and was able to go to a local school.

The moral of the story is that parents should listen to their own misgivings. We should have followed our instincts and demanded a second opinion when the hernia first developed. I often wondered how my son would have been if we had got him to the specialist hospital at 18 months.

Now that our son was physically well, the next challenge was to aid his development. The local school, although catering for mental rather than physical disability, was excellent due to an inspirational headmistress. Our son began to use objects of reference, then modest sign language. He first walked at six and began some consumption by mouth at eight. He enjoyed playing, especially with cardboard boxes. He is mentally very bright, and after three years he had really outgrown his school. My experience of finding a specialist school was depressing. The local authority refused to provide a list of possible schools. I have never understood why, but suspect that this is a control mechanism.

In my view specialist schooling for children with special educational needs is scandalously poor. Whilst there are a few outstanding and able people in this field, the general rule is that they are modest at best. Disabled children require the best teachers, not the meekest. They require a dynamic system of education and training in life skills. They require a coordinated approach from all the relevant specialities. One problem is that there is no database of best practice, trials based on sound methodology, experience, etc. Standard textbooks contain a mixture of waffle and statements of the obvious. As a result there is an element of muddling through. That said, two excellent teachers took my son through to maths GCSE.

A disabled child places a terrible strain on the parents. Being locked into the care of a disabled child tends to be all-consuming. There is little room for the couple to treat themselves or to develop their relationship. The position of other children of the family is badly distorted. As with many dads of disabled children my marriage broke down. Whilst I am not avoiding the probability that I am far from perfect (the reader may have noticed some Victor Meldrew characteristics), I believe that the root cause of the breakdown was the strain of coping. Now I am a single parent with two boys to look after, and last year I began a new chapter of experience as a single parent caring for a disabled child. It has to be said, though, that children without a disability are not too easy either.

About CHARGE association

This condition is now known as CHARGE syndrome. It was renamed on the identification of the gene mutation now known to be involved.

About half the individuals diagnosed with CHARGE syndrome have been found to have mutations of the CHD7 gene on chromosome 8. As others with the syndrome have not shown this mutation, it is thought that other genes may be involved.

The acronym CHARGE was coined to reflect the following features:

- **C**oloboma (a gap, or cleft, in one of the structures of the eye)
- **H**eart defects
- **A**tresia choanae (blockage of the nasal passages)
- **R**estricted growth and development
- **G**enital hypoplasia
- **E**ar anomalies.

Diagnosis has historically been based on fulfilling at least four out of the six diagnostic criteria in the acronym, although other features have also been variably noted.

Some of these abnormalities are more specific to CHARGE and this is now reflected in major and minor diagnostic criteria.

- **Major:** coloboma, choanal atresia, characteristic ear anomalies and cranial nerve dysfunction.

- **Minor:** include the remainder of the original features plus orofacial clefting, tracheo-oesophageal fistulae and a distinctive face.

Individuals with all four major or three major and three minor criteria undoubtedly have CHARGE, which is now considered by many to represent a discrete syndrome.

For further information see www.widerworld.co.uk/charge.

John

John is a retired doctor, living in the south-east of England. He is married with five children. His daughter, Susie, was diagnosed with meningococcal meningitis at three months old. She is now 22 and living independently.

Susannah, nearly always called Susie, our fifth child, was born normally and for the early months of her life seemed well. When she was about three months old she became unwell; she was irritable but it was difficult to pinpoint why.

As a doctor I checked her over a number of times, as did a colleague, but we could find nothing specific wrong. By the fifth day she was becoming increasingly distressed so she was admitted to hospital where meningococcal meningitis was diagnosed. We are all familiar with the dramatic picture of fulminating meningococcal septicaemia, which kills within hours, but this was an insidious illness. The rest of the family had to take preventive medication to eradicate the germ. If I had not been a doctor we would no doubt have been given clear instructions about this but no one liked to tell me what to do; however, trying to work out the drug regime for everyone else in the family at this time was difficult and stressful.

Susie made what seemed like a complete recovery but over the next few months we realised that she was no longer reacting to sounds, and by the time she was one year old we knew that she was profoundly deaf. This was established finally at a specialist centre in London, and the first consultant to look after her was very kind, patient and sympathetic. The same could not be said of his successor, whose glacial indifference to our feelings led to our contacts with this unit ceasing. The hospital had a residential unit for deaf children and their parents, and Susie and I went there together. Rosemary, my wife, had to look after the rest of the family and so was unable to come – something that was misinterpreted by the resident psychologist, who wrongly assumed that our marriage was breaking up!

Rosemary was probably more overtly distressed by the diagnosis than I; perhaps because she realised the implications more fully than I did. Our elder four children were not too upset initially, though one has said in retrospect that Susie may have diverted attention away from the other children. Friends and colleagues were mostly supportive though some, perhaps through embarrassment, seemed to ignore Susie's problem. Sensitive professionals and friends who are not frightened to talk about Susie have helped us.

At this stage hearing aids were a big problem; their great importance for a young child was emphasised but Susie emphatically rejected them, going to the most ingenious lengths to conceal them in teapots or holes in hollow trees. This was a constant source of worry to us because we wanted to do our best for her and also, it must be said, because the aids were very expensive pieces of equipment and our encounters with the insurance company were becoming increasingly embarrassing. She was also at this time becoming prematurely independent, foraging for food and not wanting to take part in family meals. There is a gentle slope at the side of our house and, on one occasion when the rest of the family were having breakfast together, we were horrified to see our car passing the window with Susie, aged three, standing on the driving seat steering, having successfully released the handbrake. Mercifully the car came to a stop without injury or damage. She was even at this age difficult to confine or discipline. A child psychiatrist whom we did not find sympathetic mentioned the possibility of autism, which horrified and depressed us; very little constructive help or support was offered to help us come to terms with this.

Susie's education started in the deaf unit at a local primary school, which could not cope with her. She then went to a school for children with multiple disabilities, where most of the children were much more disabled than her. Next she went to a school for the deaf – an appropriate placement at last but some two hours' drive away. Finally, at the age of seven, she went to a boarding school for deaf children in Margate. Rosemary and I both vividly remember taking Susie through the gates of the school for the first time. She was astonishingly composed, unlike us; I for one felt rather as a father must feel when a daughter enters a convent: she had joined the world of the deaf. In fact we should not have worried or been sad because the school was a happy place and for the first seven or eight years Susie greatly enjoyed being there. She came home for the holidays and on alternate weekends.

Integration and inclusion are often desirable objectives but this sort of language can be used to justify cheap and inadequate provision when specialised facilities are clearly needed. Deaf units in mainstream primary and secondary schools may work well for some children but this approach did not work for Susie.

Trouble began when she became a teenager. She had always had temper tantrums but as she became bigger these became more difficult to contain. Initially we were reassured that the school could cope, but a staff member was injured and Susie was abruptly expelled. There followed a time that was distressing for all concerned. Susie had enough insight to know that she had left school under a cloud, and was beside herself with grief and rage. She had to be admitted to a secure mental hospital under a compulsory order. It was difficult to find any placement for her and matters were made worse by what seemed to us like petty demarcation disputes between psychiatrists and specialists in mental handicap. The upshot was that she was sent to a unit for those with long-term learning disabilities. There were no facilities for someone with profound deafness – and in particular no signers. She was uncontrollable without medication but this contributed to her massive weight gain, which remains a problem. Social services became involved and a young social worker began a search for somewhere suitable for her to go.

After much painstaking and intelligent work she found a possible placement for her with Sense in Birmingham. This charity was originally founded for children with multiple disabilities including deafness, and they provided accommodation in a signing environment. There followed a struggle for funding, which we found hard and humiliating. We were forcibly told by one senior official that if Susie's placement was funded others would suffer – a transparent attempt to make us feel guilty. Finally, however, agreement was reached and Susie went to live at Sense, initially at the central site in the West Midlands and now in a supervised flat. Her placement there is regularly reviewed by social services and the individual social workers have always been most helpful and supportive. Susie has been as happy here as she has been anywhere, but considerable problems remain. She still has major outbursts of temper and because of her size this poses risks for her carers; it is also distressing for them, for her and indeed for us. Communication – which is by signing – is unfortunately limited and it is all too easy to see why she becomes explosively frustrated. The last time she came home was for her sister's wedding, when she had a violent outburst and broke a window, a source of great distress to her since she is very fond of her family – her bedroom is festooned with photographs of us all. We visit her every four to six weeks and, usually with some trepidation, take her out to a carvery or curry house. This can cause problems as she does behave rather strangely in public, alarming mothers with small babies by leaning into their prams, making loud noises and waving at strangers. Fortunately everyone involved has so far been very forbearing.

How has our experience changed me? Never will I let that contemptuous phrase 'welfare recipient' go unchallenged. We are in that category ourselves and the circumstances that put someone in that position are not necessarily shameful. This is a sensitive matter and social services managers need to know this. I think that dads are treated differently sometimes, as it is assumed (perhaps rightly in some cases) that we are less intimately concerned with the disabled child. It is not always appreciated that work may legitimately prevent the breadwinner attending all hospital and other appointments. This should not be misinterpreted as evidence of unconcern. Professionals need to make a point of inviting fathers to all appointments and continuing to do so even if they cannot often come. Breadwinning is difficult and important, and inability to attend every appointment does not imply a lack of concern and does not indicate a bad husband and father.

I would advise another father who has just learned that his child has a disability to keep as involved as possible. Accept that your reactions and your partner's may not always be the same; you may be more openly emotional than she, or vice versa. Don't allow this to become a source of conflict. In dealing with the authorities a combination of one obviously emotional partner and one more methodical one may be very effective!

Susie is now 22 and our hope is that she will remain with Sense in a signing environment and that, as she gets older, her frustration will diminish, her behaviour improve and her life become less restricted. My fears are around what would happen if Susie's placement were to break down and what happens when we die?

About meningococcal meningitis

Meningitis is inflammation of the meninges, the lining surrounding the brain. It can be caused by many different organisms
including bacteria, viruses, fungi and amoeba. One of the most
common causes of meningitis all over the world is the
meningococcal bacterium. The Meningitis Trust estimates that
15 per cent of sufferers are left with serious disabilities and many
more will suffer a range of short-term or less serious problems.
The length and severity of after-effects varies depending on the
type of meningitis.

For further information see www.meningitis-trust.org.

Michael

Michael is in his eighties, is retired and has a 40-year-old daughter, Sue, who has Cornelia de Lange syndrome. They both live in a coastal town in West Sussex.

I am starting to write this on my daughter Sue's birthday. On discovering that she had learning disabilities, we were warned that she might only make her teens – today she is 40 and still running. In two days' time, I will be 82 and still running.

When Sue was born she had a polyp on the gum, which necessitated an immediate operation for its removal before she could suckle. Not a good start. Mum made postnatal visits to the hospital, as did other mothers, but when she found herself going on alone she asked, 'Why am I still having to come here?' She was not told, but it did become her last visit.

When Sue was about two, we went to a local hospital because she was not attempting to speak and, during the examination, we were asked, 'Have you thought about joining Mencap?' 'Does that mean that she has learning disabilities?' we asked, although in those days we would have said 'mental handicap'. We were told 'Yes'. We remained brave, for our 11-year-old son was with us, but when we got home we retired to the bedroom and wept. Off and on we have been weeping ever since. Later, at Great Ormond Street, we learned that her syndrome was Cornelia de Lange. We attended some local meetings of Mencap, but finding there adult people with learning difficulties, we asked ourselves, 'Is this us in

20 years?' and stayed away. Later, eventually coming to terms with our situation, we went back.

As a father and breadwinner I was compelled to work (in various offices) until my retirement at age 65. Thus while Mum in the early days was trying to cope with a hyperactive child, I was at work and away from the struggle, but got caught up in helping in the evenings and at weekends. As I see it, a child's first support and defence is the mother, while the mother's first support is the father. In homes, professional carers do their shifts – and we are forever grateful to them – and then return to their private lives and normal activities, but for parents, and especially mothers, it is a 24/7 job. To find a tearful and tired mum outside the office, only being able to offer encouragement as I returned to work, was heart-wrenching.

However, at weekends, when the weather was kind, we went out into the countryside for walks, hauling the pushchair along rough tracks and over stiles. We found the great outdoors was somehow a respite and restful in its normalcy. It seemed to me, having a disabled child put us in a twilight zone; the normal chat of families was no longer for us and, as the years have rolled on, we have watched the children of friends grow to maturity and marry while Sue has remained in early childhood, and tried not to be envious.

Our holidays were taken self-catering because we could not cope with her in other establishments, and were hard work, but when she was small, I could often pick her up and carry her out of mischief. Later, however, things became more hazardous and we constantly had to be wary when approaching other innocent people. Eventually, when she went to residential school, things were easier and my duties then were being part of parents' support, attending school from time to time and taking part in their fundraising activities. My help was needed during school holidays and 'at home' weekends. I had to take days of annual leave to attend hospital with her and, when she was in a training home in Wales, take her to London to catch the train after a break. She came home willingly and mum could collect her in London, but going back required my strength and authority to get her there.

It was while she was in this residential school that our son Keith, our only other child, died in his twentieth year. Before his death he had been attending the local Gateway club as a helper and, after his demise, I volunteered to take his place. I was there for 12 years and it was only when I suffered a heart attack that I retired from this pleasurable duty. During that time I did feel that I was making some input into the well-being of other disabled people.

After Wales, things did not work out and a crisis brought a spell in a unit attached to a local mental hospital. Life for us was not smooth even though she was away from home. We needed to make frequent visits, take her out, support her and try to keep her 'motivated'. A home placement, later, worked for a while but then another crisis brought a spell in another special unit. Two more placements followed and we prayed that this time she would be settled for life, being only too conscious of our own age. But, as usual, things, after some years, went wrong and two more moves followed. For two years we travelled twice a week to visit her in the last placement, to keep her motivated and assure her that she had not been abandoned.

After the age of 16 she was supported by social workers and the NHS learning disability team. They found placements for her when needed and made regular visits. One of the NHS team has now known her for 20 years. She eventually came within the orbit of a specialist charity and we found there a wonderfully supporting group who, in spite of yet another failure, have continued to help her. With their help, and the backing of social services, Sue has been provided with a place of her own. We will be eternally grateful to them – and feel that we, in our old age, are being supported too. Now, in her own flat in town, which we helped to prepare and furnish, and with full supervision, we see her most weeks for coffee and have her home for the day on a Saturday. Now we are looking for a settled time for us – but, from past experience, who can say that this is it?

Since my retirement I have been able to give more help and support, although with eyesight problems I can no longer drive a car and that has created fresh difficulties. During periods of tiredness and depression I sometimes feel that 40 years is equivalent to two life sentences and still ongoing, but in general, would not think of pulling out or shedding my responsibilities. Fathers should never walk away and leave mothers to cope on their own. In marriage we made the promise 'for better, for worse' and should stick by that – not only by contract but also by love and understanding. I do wonder, however, about today's partnering as a form of marriage and whether there can be the same commitment. Perhaps there is and I am just old-fashioned, but we are all conditioned in our early years, which sets a personal pattern for life. In spite of my moans and groans we have had – and still have – good times. Although our milestones may be only yards apart, we still delight in the reaching of new goals, even at 40.

About Cornelia de Lange syndrome

Cornelia de Lange syndrome (CdLS) is rare and affects between 1 in 15,000 and 1 in 50,000 babies born.

Children with the syndrome are small at birth and remain small compared to children of the same age. The children will have slow or very slow development, usually associated with significant learning problems that are of variable severity. Some children have psychological and behavioural problems including autistic-like features and self-injury. Most children have some form of limb abnormality but these can range from having small hands and particularly short thumbs in mild cases to an almost complete absence of the forearms in severe cases. Almost all children will have an unusual marbled appearance to the skin on their arms and legs, particularly when they are cold. The most striking feature of the syndrome is that all the children look alike, like brothers and sisters. Some medical complications are very common in CdLS including feeding and bowel problems (particularly gastro-oesophageal reflux), and hearing problems.

For further information see www.cdls.org.uk.

Conclusion

Getting the help you need

One of the most important messages that comes across from the dads that have talked to us in the preceding pages comes from John; his succinct advice is not to panic and to try to believe that it's not the end of the world. Kevin's advice is straightforward: 'Enjoy it mate.' When you first start to realise that something is wrong, or first receive a diagnosis, it can be tempting to think that it is the end of all your hopes and dreams for your child. What these stories tell us is that this isn't the case. You may need to develop new hopes and dreams, but these will come.

Most of the dads felt that one of their most important needs was information, but dads like Simon and Paul also remind us that the information needs to be interpreted in the light of your own child as each child is unique, regardless of the diagnosis. As your child grows you may be able to take a great deal of pleasure in what they can do and focus less on what they can't, as Jonathon and several of the other dads advise. Andrew tells us that being proud of your child is key, and Jonathon reminds us that we need to accept our children as they are and not dwell on how we would like them to be.

Don't be afraid to be a pain in the backside, as Phil tells us, in your search for the information that you need, but try to adopt a collaborative rather than 'us and them' approach.

Having a sense of humour is important, as Simon tells us. And John advises not to mind people staring. Patience is also a virtue that you may need to acquire…

Being listened to, to have someone that can just be a sounding block for you, is important. We urge you to try to make use of all your own support networks – it might be your wife or partner, friend or neighbour.

It might be helpful to try and just get some time to yourself or spend some time alone with your partner. Remember that it's OK to ask for help.

John tells us that mums and dads may react differently, but that this can be a strength in the battles to come. Standing by your partner and talking are highlighted by both Rob and Michael. And, even if you separate, Jonathon reminds us of the importance of putting your own differences aside and acting in the interests of your child.

Going out or pursuing your own interests might cause a few difficulties but, if you do, it can make all the difference to how you feel about your situation. Rob's rugby really helped him let off steam and the country walks that Michael and his family enjoyed gave them a feeling of peace. Having some time together as a couple can be really valuable, so make use of any help that might be available. Some dads, like Mike, found a special activity that only they did with their child, and that became 'their' time; for Mike it was trampolining and swimming. Rob describes his pleasure in being able to continue to carry Matthew even when he became bigger, as it was something only he could do. Steve found an escape and some quiet time in playing with his games console.

The wider family can be a useful support, although not all parents have found them to be. Jonathon and Steve told us how much their families had helped by giving them a break or helping with DIY, for example. Several of the dads spoke movingly about the value of true friends. Andrew's description of how his colleagues supported him through depression is a reminder of how much workmates can play a part in coping. Rob advises dads not to waste time 'chasing the vanished', but to enjoy the real friends who stay the course. Nigel shows us that sometimes other people can need help to understand how to respond appropriately, but also how much support can be gained from a faith community.

Some of the dads, like Gordon, had a complete career change to fit in around their new responsibilities; others, like Matthew, altered their hours; and some, like Kevin, gave up work altogether. It is important to find a job and a work pattern that suits you. Richard and Phil's stories illustrate how sometimes having the wonderful career and all the trappings is not the be all and end all, and that concentrating more on family life can be just as, or more, satisfying.

Support groups around disability might be a good way of meeting other parents who are in a similar situation, who 'get it' – as only parents who are in the same situation really can. Even if you do not want to go to a support group when your child is first diagnosed or don't find it helpful, like Michael, like him you could go back when the time is right for you.

Some dads, like Mike and Simon, found that getting involved in campaigning for better rights for disabled people helped them. In Tony's case, political activities gave him a more broad focus on a variety of causes.

Support groups for those dealing with specific conditions can also give you all the basic information you need, although it does need to be interpreted in the light of your own child. Both mums and dads can join support groups, and there are also a growing number of dads' support groups as many organisations wake up to the need to support dads. Similarly, support groups don't have to be focused just on sitting and talking. Two dads told Contact a Family about a football team they have set up for their children. This has a double advantage: the children get access to sport and, whilst they are playing, their parents get to talk to each other.

Even if there is not a support group in your area, if you have access to the Internet you can chat to other parents anonymously across the world via Contact a Family's Website: www.makingcontact.org. The site currently works in English, Arabic, Mandarin, Somali and Farsi, and more languages are planned.

If there is no support group for the condition your child is affected by, you could start one, as Andrew did.

A national organisation for parents or carers might be a good place to start. Depending on where you live the following would be worth looking at.

UK
Contact a Family
www.cafamily.org.uk

Australia
Carers Australia
www.carersaustralia.com.au

Canada
Canadian Organization for Rare Disorders
www.raredisorders.ca

Europe

European Organization for Rare Disorders
www.eurordis.org

New Zealand

Parent to Parent New Zealand
www.parent2parent.org.nz

Carers NewZealand
www.carers.net.nz

USA

National Organization for Rare Disorders (NORD)
www.rarediseases.org

Knowing your rights

Knowing your rights is also very important. Many countries have legislation around employment rights for parents, for example. Many have some kind of benefits or social security provision. Rob and Tony remind us of the importance of knowing your rights, pushing and not taking no for an answer. John advises parents to get a second opinion and to question everything, and Edward also stresses the importance of trusting your instincts and listening to your own misgivings. Mike and Yuri stress that it is very important to try to attend important meetings about your child's future.

Richard's story reminds us that parents know what kind of help will suit their child best, and that seeing your Member of Parliament, complaining and seeking legal help if necessary can work in getting the provision that your child needs.

Although the type of provision will vary depending on the country that you live in, what almost certainly won't vary is the bureaucracy that you will be confronted with when you need help, as Tony's battles for education and support demonstrate. For this reason, it would be our advice to start looking for information about your rights and how to enforce them as early as you can face it. Don't wait until you are at crisis point to start enquiring about respite care and short breaks, and don't wait until you are close to destitute before finding out about the benefits you can claim. It is likely that this sort of provision will take at least weeks, if not months, to access.

A local or national disability organisation or patient group might be a good place to start, and will certainly be able to point you in the right direction. If you have access to the Internet, you can also find a lot of information on your local or national government website.

The UK charity Contact a Family's website (www.cafamily.org.uk), for example, has information on all the main social security benefits that can be claimed, social care and health service provision, adaptations and equipment for children, employment rights, and a host of other information.

What can services do for fathers?

There are some key messages here for those that work in or provide services. Services, meetings and training need to be arranged at a time when both parents might have the opportunity to attend. Fathers may have a different, but equally valuable, view to offer.

At all Contact a Family's fathers' events we ask, 'What would you say to professionals?' Consistent themes have emerged:

- services/professionals tend to ignore fathers and talk to mothers
- it's hard for a dad to get a meeting one-to-one, but sometimes dads want to talk to you alone
- meetings are always in the day when we are at work
- we are made to feel like the enforcers, the hard men, who just turn up to shout when things go wrong, and we don't want to have to always do this
- sometimes we don't feel strong
- have services for dads rather than services for mums that dads can use
- be seen to want us dads to come to events and meetings
- don't make us feel stupid when we ask questions
- don't make us feel as though we are there to make up the numbers
- don't lie to us, even if you think the truth may be hurtful
- treat us with respect.

Sometimes very simple things can make a difference – for example, Matthew spoke of his irritation that, despite the fact that he was the one who took Joseph to the hospital, follow-up letters would always arrive addressed to his wife.

Kash reminds us of the importance of treating fathers with emotional respect, and looking beyond the anger that some parents may express to appreciate that they are only trying to access support and help for their families.

A lot of the dads we met and spoke to felt that services did not meet their needs as fathers, and some almost went as far as completely excluding them. One dad who was tired of meetings being arranged in the daytime said, 'Services need to be more flexible; they need to arrange home visits outside the hours of 9 am to 5 pm.' Many dads felt very strongly about the way they were treated. Here are some of the things they said:

- 'When we have a doctor's appointment, she only talks to my wife.'
- 'I would love to go to all the meetings but I just can't.'
- 'They see you as a necessary evil. They seem really wary of dads. There is something really big at stake if dad walks in.'
- 'They seem shocked if we as fathers ask questions.'
- 'The professionals presume you are not involved with your child just because you aren't present at the meeting.'
- 'Because I have to go to work they think it's a rest. They don't see that you are the one living with the child.'
- 'We're seen as being a dad for the day if mum is not there. Professionals are not acknowledging what goes on out of hours.'
- 'My wife has had training on lifting and handling, but I was not offered it. I lift him too. It seems that training is not for dads but we give personal care too.'
- 'Both parents can't always be there [at meetings] – I might miss vital information because my wife focuses on the negative things that are said.'

If you are reading this book because you are working as, or training to be, a social worker, a teacher, a nurse or any one of the caring professions, we hope that you have gained some understanding of the dad's perspective. The need for sensitivity and honesty around the time of diagnosis shines through from many of these dads' accounts. And as a professional, listening, treating families with respect and simple human kindness can make such an enormous difference. Many of the dads in this book remember individual workers who were especially helpful, years and even decades after their contact with them ceased.

There are lots of things you can do to involve both mothers and fathers in the design of your service, and voluntary organisations would usually be happy to advise you how you might go about doing this.

The message from these men is: 'think dad'. Don't forget to ask dads if they need any further information; offer them a number they can ring outside working hours to get information if they need to. And, if you do nothing else, please tell them to get hold of a copy of this book.

We leave the last words to dads and they can apply equally to fathers and those who work with them:

Be positive, be proud. You are all heroes in your own right.

Glossary of terms

What follows is an alphabetical list of words and phrases used in the text that may be unfamiliar to readers (we have also included some colloquial phrases used in the dads' accounts, which may be unfamiliar to readers outside the UK).

Acoustically to do with sound or hearing.

Aorta main artery that carries blood from the heart to the body.

Atresia blocked or missing.

Bairn a colloquial word for child.

Behaviour modification a general term to describe techniques for changing a child's behaviour. An example of behaviour modification is punishment and reward.

Benign usually not dangerous or life threatening.

Bilateral disc hernia a condition in which a part of the disc found in the spine pushes through the fibrous band that normally binds it. In a bilateral condition, both the left and right side are affected. This usually occurs low in the back, and can cause severe pain.

Biopsy examination of tissue.

Blood oxygen saturation the amount of oxygen in the blood.

Breech position breech birth is the delivery of the unborn baby rear end first.

Bronchialitis a chest infection caused by a virus; occurs in babies. It can leave the baby coughing and wheezing for many months or even years following the infection.

Caesarean section a surgical procedure where the baby is removed via an opening that has been cut into the abdomen. This usually happens when a natural birth would lead to complications.

Cannula a hollow needle inserted into a blood vessel and used to give intravenous fluids or drugs.

Cardiologist doctor who specialises in conditions of the heart.

Carer's Allowance a UK benefit paid to someone who looks after a disabled child or adult.

Central nervous system composed of the brain, spinal cord and the associated nerves, the CNS is the control network for the entire body.

Cerebral palsy a disorder caused by a brain injury that occurred before or during birth, or in the first few months after birth. Damage may cause paralysis (palsy) in one or more parts of the body, limited motor skills, speech difficulties, learning disabilities or other problems.

Chromosome a rod-like structure present in the nucleus of all body cells (with the exception of the red blood cells), which stores genetic information. Normally, humans have a total of 46 (23 pairs).

Clinical geneticist a health professional who specialises in inherited and other genetic disorders.

Congenital a disease or condition with which someone is born.

Contra-indications a term used to refer to medical conditions in which a product should not be used (for example, 'You should not take this medicine if you are pregnant').

Community nurse a nurse who works to provide health support at the patient's home.

Cranial osteopathy an alternative therapy where the osteopath uses her or his hands to manipulate bones, particularly in the head, to treat various disorders.

Crash/resuscitation team a group of health professionals who are brought in to try to restore heart rhythm and breathing when a patient has lost consciousness.

Crystal, David a well-known writer, lecturer and broadcaster on language and linguistics.

Cyst an abnormal mass in the body containing a liquid or semi-solid substance.

Dilatation widening of an opening.

Direct payments UK families who are able to get support from social services may choose to receive cash instead, to buy their own care.

Disability Living Allowance a UK benefit paid to disabled children and adults who have mobility problems or need additional care or supervision.

Double incontinence inability to control the flow of urine from the bladder (urinary incontinence) and the escape of stools from the rectum (faecal incontinence).

Early years centre somewhere that can give parents information about children's services in their area.

ECG electrocardiogram – a test that measures the electrical activity of the heart muscle.

ECMO extra corporeal membrane oxygenation – a treatment to support the heart or lung. With ECMO, blood from the baby's vein is pumped through an artificial heart/lung where oxygen is added and carbon dioxide removed. The blood is then returned back to the baby.

Education Appeal Tribunal now called *SENDIST* (see separate entry).

Education Authority the part of UK local government that is responsible for planning education in an area.

Educational psychologist a person who uses psychological theory to assess children with learning difficulties and advise on their development and educational progress.

Educationalist a specialist in the theory of education and different ways to teach.

EEG electroencephalography – a test used to detect and record the electrical activity generated by the brain.

Endocrinologist a doctor who specialises in diseases related to the glands of the endocrine system (e.g. the thyroid, pancreas and adrenal glands).

Epidural medication injected around the spinal cord during labour to reduce pain.

Every Child Matters a new government policy approach to the well-being of children and young people from birth to age 19 in England.

Facial palsy paralysis of the muscles in the face.

Family centre a local centre for children to socialise in a safe environment, providing opportunities for mutual support and self-help amongst parents.

Fundoplication surgical procedure that ties the top of the stomach around the oesophagus to prevent reflux.

Gastronomy button a device inserted into the stomach to decompress it.

Genetic syndrome/disorder a disorder that is inherited or caused by a gene.

Gestation the time a baby is in the womb.

Global neurodevelopmental delay when two or more stages in early childhood development are slowed down or missed out.

GP abbreviation for General Practitioner. A doctor who provides care in a surgery or clinic to patients registered under the NHS.

Grommet a tiny pipe that is put across the eardrum, which helps to drain any fluid and lets air into the middle ear.

Gynaecologist a doctor who specialises in the investigation and treatment of the female reproductive organs and functions.

Hackney carriage driver a taxi driver who drives a traditional hackney carriage, or 'black cab'.

Haemorrhaging bleeding; loss of blood.

Heart echo mechanic an echocardiogram (often called 'echo') is a graphic outline of the heart's movement. The heart echo mechanic, or sonographer, uses ultrasound to evaluate the pumping action of the heart.

Heterogeneous dissimilar.

Hiatus hernia an upwards protrusion of the stomach through the diaphragm wall.

Hospice an establishment that cares for people who are facing the end of life.

Huff, go off in a move away in a sulky, bad-tempered manner.

Hypoplastic underdeveloped.

Incapacity Benefit a UK benefit for adults who are too ill or disabled to work (shortly to be replaced by Employment and Support Allowance).

Income Support a UK means-tested benefit for those with insufficient money to live on.

Intubation insertion of a tube through the nose or mouth into the trachea (windpipe).

Jejunostomy the surgical formation of an opening through the abdominal wall into the jejunum (a section of the small intestine).

Judicial review a form of UK court proceeding in which a judge reviews the lawfulness of a decision or action made by a public body.

Kick off start to get angry.

Legal aid help with legal fees in the UK for those on a modest income.

Makaton a system of communication using a combination of spoken words, sign language vocabulary and graphic symbols. It is primarily used as a communication medium by children and adults with learning disabilities.

Meldrew, Victor a UK TV sitcom character well known for raging against the petty annoyances of life.

Meningitis a condition in which inflammation of the meninges (lining) of the brain and spinal cord occurs due to a bacterial, viral or, rarely, fungal infection.

Meningococcal septicaemia blood poisoning caused by the meningococcal bacteria.

Merosin a group of substances that are involved in the repair and development of muscle tissue.

Mitral the mitral valve is situated between the atrium and ventricle (chambers on the left of the heart).

MMR jab measles, mumps and rubella vaccination.

Motor skills the ability to use muscles effectively. Gross motor skills include lifting your head, sitting up, balancing, crawling and walking, while fine motor skills include manipulating small objects, transferring objects from hand to hand, and various hand–eye coordination tasks, etc.

MRSA abbreviation for either multiple antibiotic resistant staphylococcus aureus or methicillyn antibiotic resistant staphylococcus aureus. If a patient is infected with this bacteria it is difficult to cure because of its resistance to antibiotics.

Nasal/naso-gastric tube a plastic tube inserted through the nose into the stomach to feed patients who are unable to eat normally.

Neonatal the first four weeks after a child's birth.

Neurologist a specialist who diagnoses and treats disorders of the nervous system.

NHS the National Health Service is the system of delivering health care in the United Kingdom. It was set up in 1948 and is now the largest health service organisation in Europe.

Occupational therapist a health professional trained to evaluate and help people who are ill or disabled learn to manage their daily activities.

Oesophageal atresia a rare condition where a short section at the top of the *oesophagus* (gullet) doesn't develop properly. This can mean that food cannot pass from the throat to the stomach.

Oesophagus the portion of the intestine that runs from the throat to the stomach, also known as the 'gullet'.

Ophthalmologist a doctor specialising in eye disorders and treatment.

Paediatric cardiologist a doctor specialising in heart disorders and treatment in children.

Paediatric consultant a medical specialist who gives advice on and treatment for conditions affecting children.

Perinatal the period around birth (five months before and one month after).

Picture Exchange Communication System a system where a child with language impairment is taught to exchange a picture for an item they want.

Pethidine a very strong painkiller.

Physiotherapy a health care profession concerned with human function and movement, and maximising potential.

Pint, go for a have an alcoholic drink.

Plastic exoskeletons/splints a rigid support designed to hold bones in place to allow healing, or to prevent movement in general.

Portage a UK home-visiting educational service for preschool children with additional support needs and their families.

Prenatal the time before birth while a baby is developing during pregnancy.

Prozac a medication used to treat a number of mental disorders, intended to improve the mood and feelings of the patient by restoring the balance of natural substances in the brain.

Psychiatrist a medical doctor who specialises in the diagnosis and treatment of emotional and mental disorders. Unlike a *psychologist*, they can prescribe medicine.

Psychologist a non-medical specialist who can talk with patients and their families to help them overcome emotional, mental and personal matters.

Psychotherapy types of treatments that involve talking and listening to treat mental health or emotional conditions.

Reflux the term used when liquid backs up into the *oesophagus* from the stomach.

Respite care a short break from looking after a disabled child or adult, usually arranged through social services or sometimes the NHS.

Rispiradone a drug used to treat certain mental/mood disorders. This medication is sometimes used to treat autistic children, and is intended to help them think clearly and function in daily life.

Ritalin a stimulant medication used to treat attention deficit hyperactivity disorder (ADHD).

SENDIST the Special Needs & Disability Tribunal hears appeals against decisions made by local education authorities in England about special educational needs and disability matters.

Social services/social work department the part of UK local government that is responsible for the welfare of disabled children (and other vulnerable groups).

Special care baby unit a part of the hospital that provides care for low-weight babies in the first few weeks after they are born.

Special Educational Needs Register a list of children in a school who have special educational needs for which specific measures are taken and monitored.

Statement of Special Educational Needs a document written about a child (in England, Wales or Northern Ireland), which obliges the relevant education authorities to provide specific help at school.

Stenosis narrowing, often of a blood vessel.

Supply teaching teaching on a temporary contract, usually to cover short- or long-term vacancies, sick leave or maternity leave.

Tracheomalcia a weakness and floppiness of the walls of the trachea (main airway).

Trachie tracheotomy is the surgical creation of an artificial airway in the trachea (windpipe). A tube can be inserted to hold the hole open and this is known as a tracheostomy, or trachie.

Ventricle a small cavity or chamber within a body or organ, especially the chamber on the left side of the heart that receives arterial blood.

Viral pneumonia pneumonia caused by a virus.

Wall, go up the become really furious, have a temper tantrum.

Index